Embracing and Healing Your Wounded Inner Child

Practical Steps to Overcome Past Trauma and Restore Inner Peace

Kieran Garza

Table of Contents

Trigger Warning

Trigger warning: This book delves into sensitive topics, including mental health disorders, physical and verbal abuse, and suicide. Reader discretion is advised as the content may be triggering or upsetting for individuals who have experienced trauma or are sensitive to these subjects. Take care of yourself and seek support if needed while engaging with this material.

Introduction

I'd been going back and forth with this woman for nearly 15 minutes. Her children clung to their father and sobbed uncontrollably. Him: speechless. The negotiation was failing fast and I needed to get in there. Banging down the door, my team and I rushed in.

"Don't come any closer!"

"Ma'am, look at me; whatever you're going through, this is not the answer—no!"

My screams echoed in my head, and the sight of the blood-drenched bathtub became eternally imprinted in my mind. *What would make someone seemingly so happy to do something this grotesque?*

"Stay with me!" I pleaded.

Grabbing every towel I could find, I hurriedly pulled her from the tub and rested her on the floor. My colleague joined in, attempting to stop the bleeding.

1

"Do you know who you are?" I asked.

Nodding, she said, "Just let me die."

I refused to let her go. Trying to keep her conscious, I began talking, attempting to get to the reasons behind it all. The tears streamed from her face as she shared the emotional torment she'd been trapped in.

I'd been doing this job for a long time and never before had I felt such sheer horror as I did that day. A beautiful suburban wife and mother of three had **mutilated** herself in her bathtub. She suffered from depression in the past but according to everyone who knew her, she worked through it. She knew how much it meant to those who loved her to see her mental health improve, but the secrets of her past trauma haunted her every day of her life. Feeling **isolated** and misunderstood, she turned to the only thing she thought could put an end to it.

As a first responder, I deal with physical emergencies on a regular basis yet it took that moment for me to realize that these events are, more often than not, the **byproduct** of deep-seated emotional trauma. Many people have no idea how to free themselves from the shackles of past **anguish**. So much so that they either develop consistently destructive habits throughout their adulthood or suffer in silence—until one day, they crumble.

Unfortunately, many people are unfamiliar with the concept of the *wounded inner child*. This concept is a profound one—a recognition that the pain we experience in adulthood is often rooted in unresolved trauma from our earlier years. Like a **dormant** seed buried deep within the soil of our subconscious, these childhood wounds lie dormant, waiting to be awakened by the storms of life. Most times, we fail to make the connection between events from our childhood and our perceptions, actions, and reactions as adults. And this reality is one that cannot be overlooked any longer.

Long-Term Effects of Childhood Trauma

Our brains are responsible for processing, interpreting, and acting on information provided by internal and external influencers. This is achieved through the development and communication between **neurons** in the brain network. Unfortunately, trauma can not only impact the functions of our brain systems; it can completely alter the structure of our brain as well as the pattern of interpreting information.

Early childhood brain development sets the tone for future growth as the rapid formation of neural pathways relies on repeated exposure to certain situations as a means to program the brain's responses. Needless to say, repeated exposure to highly stressful situations results in excessive or overuse of trauma-related brain functions, which focus development on those areas of the brain and reduce or **hinder** development in other important areas of the brain. This can cause significant neurological damage and delays and cause victims to develop an inability to **regulate** their own emotions (N.C. Division of Social Services and the Family and Children's Resource Program, 2012).

For this reason, healing our inner child is vital to our overall well-being. With healing comes the transformative power of emotional **liberation** and resilience. I have witnessed firsthand how the wounds of the past can **manifest** in the present, casting a shadow over even the happiest moments. By confronting the pain of our past and nurturing the wounded child within us, we unlock a fountain of strength that empowers us to navigate life's challenges with courage. We open new doors of opportunity and growth when we allow ourselves to open up to the beauty of healing by confronting our demons as opposed to running from them.

Admittedly, this road may be one of many struggles, harsh truths, and revisiting some painful moments that many of us would much rather pretend never existed; however, the finish line will bring more reward than you can imagine. Sure, this ride will be a rollercoaster of a ride, and undoing years' worth of damage can seem impossible, but I'm here to show you just how possible it is. The key is getting started, staying committed, and finding **solace** in the fact that you are not alone.

And so, it is with a sense of purpose and **conviction** that we embark on this journey—a journey to guide you in recognizing, confronting, and healing your own inner child wounds. Through the sharing of my own experiences, the exploration of key concepts, and the practice of healing exercises, you will be guided step-by-step on the path to reclaiming your inner child and unlocking the true essence of your being.

Now, without further ado, let the transformation begin!

Chapter 1:

The Wounded Inner Child

For most people, there is no deeper meaning behind certain likes and dislikes, **quirks** and habits, or even **preconceived** opinions or perspectives they have. This couldn't be further from the truth. In fact, everything we experience from the time we enter this world up until the time we depart plays a crucial role in who we become.

Sure, some experiences leave more lasting impressions on us than others, but we are nothing if not a collection or **summation** of all our life's events. That said, experiences that occur during the earlier stages of our lives lay the primary foundation for the individuals we become, which is why most traumas that take place during this time carry the most weight in our character development. I know some people will consider this concept and dismiss it since there's a **stigma**, of sorts, attached to a wounded inner child. One that suggests that in order for your inner child to be wounded, extreme abuse, neglect, or general exposure to violence would need to be **prevalent** to lead to becoming a damaged adult. In reality, there are a variety of experiences and events that can cause permanent wounds, and the quicker we acknowledge and accept this, the easier it will be to start the healing process.

In this chapter, I'd like us to **venture** into the depths of what the wounded inner child really means and how to recognize the signs. You might be seeing things a little differently after this, and we'll be able to uncover how it all started as well as how those events have impacted your adult life. This is an essential first step on the road to recovery, healing, and liberation.

Understanding Your Inner Child

Unraveling the core reasons behind the traumatized inner child in you can be a difficult task, especially if you're convinced that there is no depth behind who you are and have become. I've already mentioned that we all have an inner child. This isn't something negative; it's simply our emotional core, which is established and developed during childhood.

Your emotional core is responsible for your perception of others and the world around you, as well as how you handle and react to certain situations. Let's say, for instance, that you're a workaholic, and any time someone points out a mistake, no matter how small, you become overcome with anxiety, humiliation, and even a sense of hopelessness. This would typically indicate that your inner child may be scarred by the reactions or consequences of making a mistake as a child and that, as an adult, you make it your mission to do everything perfectly—often to the point of obsession. To highlight my point of our inner child's influence not being limited to negative experiences and emotions, let's look at a positive example. You might be someone, or have met someone, who is obsessed with the holidays. Everything, from the twinkling lights to the smell of warm, buttery cookies fresh out of the oven, gets you all warm and fuzzy inside. This is the result of the experiences that shaped your inner child.

6

Case Study

Jada, a friend of mine, had a severely wounded inner child, and it wasn't until I pointed it out that she took a step back, assessed her behaviors, and made the connection with her childhood. She had a serious issue with lights being on in her house at night after going to bed. Now, it's important to know that some people like having one light, like the bathroom or passage light, on during the night, and some people don't. Just because you don't like the lights on at night is not a sign of a wounded inner child. The reason this was the case for her **transcends** the mere act of keeping a light or two on at night.

Her father was a violent alcoholic and worked late hours in his garage, so when he'd get home at night, everyone would be asleep and all the lights were off. As soon as the lights went on, they knew trouble would **ensue**. The sound of her mother being **yanked** from her bed still makes Jada's skin crawl. After discovering how and why that **inexplicable** fear and anxiety surface when the lights come on at night, she was able to begin the journey of reclaiming her life. The first thing she did was explain these **complexities** to her partner since they'd had countless arguments about him forgetting to turn off all the lights at night and he began viewing this outrageous **phobia** as an obsession that would eventually bring their relationship to its knees. Of course, this was one of many other little, inexplicable quirks and since it could often not be explained, it, in turn, made it impossible for the other person to understand.

Once she laid everything out for her partner, he supported her through every aspect of her recovery. Whether it was in therapy or employing activities that slowly **redefined** what certain situations meant to her, they did it all. You have to be willing to acknowledge that there is damage to be repaired in the first place; only then can you take the necessary steps to rebirth.

How Childhood Trauma Affects You

The way in which childhood trauma leaves its mark on your physical and mental well-being differs from person to person. As much as we don't want to accept that there's something **fundamentally** different about us as a result of our wounds, we need to acknowledge this reality if we plan to change it.

Disconnect or Dissociation

This refers to an **adaptive** ability formed as a result of **perpetual** exposure to intense emotions. Emotions that we may not have been ready or capable of dealing with at the time it occurred. So, in order to protect ourselves, we develop the ability to disconnect from reality and those specific emotions and numb ourselves until we are ready to reconnect with our present surroundings again. In some cases, individuals master **dissociation** to the extent of disconnecting entirely from their own identities.

The disconnect can last anywhere from a few minutes to a few weeks, depending on the state of mind of the person experiencing it. Many times, dissociation can be treated with various forms of self-therapy; however, when dissociation **morphs** into a dissociative disorder, professional **intervention** is recommended.

Signs of Dissociative Disorder

- **compulsive** behaviors that are out of your control

- difficulty staying focused

- **lapses** in memory even when you had no physical head injury or medical reason for it

- feeling like life or certain events are unreal

- feeling like you're watching yourself live but you're not feeling like you're living

- abrupt shifts in mood

- frequent, unmanageable emotions

- trouble with your own identity (acting in ways unlike yourself)

- severe anxiety and depression

Psychological Disorders

Trauma has a way of rearranging your personality for the worse. Feelings that were meant to come and go remain and **embed** themselves in the core of your being and you **inadvertently** process those reactions as a part of your identity. You feel trapped in a cycle of negative thought processes that eventually progress into disorders that now require treatment and sometimes medication. The psychological disorders commonly related to trauma include Post-Traumatic Stress Disorder (PTSD), social anxiety disorders, Borderline Personality Disorder (BPD), panic disorders, generalized anxiety disorders, and more.

Some people spend their entire lives suffering the consequences of their trauma and their minds literally become their living nightmare. **Prolonged** exposure to these types of disorders can result in **insomnia**, respiratory and heart problems, and digestive issues.

Destructive Coping Mechanisms

Continued **victimization** often causes victims to resort to destructive habits like substance abuse, self-harm, harming others, and **promiscuity**. These are but a handful of the destructive coping mechanisms established to help you not only get through the traumatic event but they are usually also done to numb future exposure. Not only do these habits by themselves have adverse effects, but they can also lead to extreme guilt and **self-loathing**, which in turn creates a ripple effect and sets off a series of further destructive actions.

Recognizing the Signs of Wounds

While it's true that our inner child stimulates many positive emotions and reactions, I'd like to highlight some of the less appealing signs. This will make it easier to establish whether your inner child is screaming for help or not. These may be as follows:

- abandonment issues

- codependency

- poor body image

- feelings of worthlessness

- prioritizing pleasing others

- harsh inner critic

- addicted to conflict, chaos, and rebellion

- ruminating thoughts

- **catastrophizing**

- need for control

- trust issues

- commitment issues

- inability to be vulnerable

- feeling like a misfit

- fear of expressing yourself

- fear of change

- depression

- inexplicable anger or rage

- fear of setting boundaries

- irrational connection to objects (hoarding)

- inconsistency in completing tasks

- overachieving

- perfectionism

- constantly feeling unsafe

- irrational fear of confrontation or conflict

- **procrastination**

I know that nearly everyone we know shows signs of at least one of these. The thing is, these symptoms, even individually, convey that there is already something fundamentally **imbalanced** in our **psyche** and some of them could just be a result of external factors. That said, in most cases, it all boils down to the wounded inner child.

As much as your inner child can connect the smell of freshly baked bread with holidays at grandpa and grandma's house, they can also connect the smell of beer and cigarettes to the awful nights spent in fear and misery when mom had to leave you with the neighbor because she was working late. Only when you know which of these signs are present within yourself, then you can effectively strategize ways to overcome them. I've seen countless people fall into the trap of cutting all ties with their inner child to avoid having to deal with those emotions at all. This is because the pain experienced was so severe that burying it deep within their **subconscious** is the only way that they'd be able to carry on. It goes without saying that this tactic is like placing a rotten egg in a basket and covering and surrounding it with fresh eggs. Eventually, that single rotten egg will spoil every last egg in the basket, one by one.

Now, simply looking at these signs might still leave you second-guessing whether this really is you, so have a look at the below questions that you can ask yourself, and if the answer to any of them is yes, then consider your inner child: wounded.

Does change make me anxious, depressed, or irrationally fearful?

Am I lying to others, and sometimes to myself, when I say that I trust them?

Do I feel like the world can swallow me whole when I mess up?

Do I think people who want to spend time with me have an ulterior motive?

Am I always searching for more in life?

Do I feel ugly no matter what I do?

Is starting a task or finishing a task impossible for me?

Do I feel like people are always judging me?

Am I always thinking, "What if?"

Am I afraid to be alone?

Do I avoid conflict, even if it means being unhappy with a situation?

Am I constantly seeking out thrills and adrenaline to feel alive?

Do I need to be a few steps ahead of everybody and everything all the time?

Am I afraid to commit to someone because I think they will disappoint me, or will I disappoint them?

Answer these questions honestly, and I assure you that a huge weight will be lifted from your shoulders. You will finally be letting your wounded inner child know that you hear them and that you're ready to face them.

Case Study

Ava, a young lady I met while on duty, serves as a striking example. A successful 24-year-old junior manager at a financial agency, displaying traits of an overachiever. She **ingested** a significant amount of her grandmother's pills in an attempt to harm herself. Although saving her life required immense effort, I am grateful to have been able to do so. I revisited her case, as it remained puzzling to me.

"What was going on in your head?" I asked as I sat beside her hospital bed.

"Have you ever been so tired that you'd rather die than do another task?" She asked in response.

It wasn't her question that struck me; it was the expression of utter defeat on her face. *How could a 24-year-old feel worn out by life?* We spoke for about two hours. This young lady possessed a captivating intellect with an extraordinary **affinity** for numbers and patterns. Her talents were recognized at a young age, leading her parents to **exploit** her abilities. At the age of 10, she assisted in expanding the family business, assuming responsibility for **meticulous** oversight to prevent errors. Her reputation as a **prodigy** spread, attracting numerous clients to the family enterprise.

She was denied the opportunity to engage in playful activities or simply be a child, as her family relied on her exceptional intellect. Initially, she felt honored. Proud of her uniqueness, she nurtured an **insatiable** ambition. However, the desire to contribute more only increased the demands placed on her. Rest was a luxury she was never afforded.

She was exhausted and felt left with no option but to escape the shackles of the family business. After joining a small firm, she thought her days of mind-numbing number crunching were behind her, but it turned out the firm only hired her because of her **distinguished** track record. It was then that she decided that this so-called gift would trail her wherever she went.

"I will never be free," she lamented.

Assuming the responsibility of guiding her toward self-discovery and recovery, I introduced group therapy, creative outlets, and more. Today, she's an exceptional artist. She paints breathtaking landscapes in the solace of her home, far from the exploitation and greed of those who want to **deplete** her strength.

Tracing the Origins

Figuring out the birthplace of our wounds is an essential part of reducing, and eventually eliminating, factors that can trigger negative emotional responses. Of course, if you've spent a lifetime, inadvertently or intentionally, drowning out your inner child, tracing the trauma that shaped you can be really difficult—though not impossible.

This is not going to be easy and you need to be ready for some raw, overwhelming emotions, but when done correctly, this will be the beginning of your transformation. Remember that it's better to heal one day at a time than to diminish one day at a time. And that's exactly what **repressing** your issues will do. The internal **torment** you experience by trying to hold onto your relationships while ignoring the cause behind the problems in them can completely alter your personality and even your brain chemistry.

Have a look at the below therapy, as it is an effective and, more importantly, safe way to explore your past.

Guided Imagery

Guided imagery is a form of therapy typically used to induce relaxation and relieve stress; however, it can also be used as a tool to revisit childhood memories and uncover the events that shaped the core of our being. While it can be performed by a professional **psychotherapist**, we can also train ourselves to do it.

Here's a step-by-step guide on how to perform your own guided imagery therapy:

1. Get as comfortable as possible (you can sit on a meditation pillow or lay on the bed). It can also help to have scents or articles in your space that remind you of your childhood.

2. Gently close your eyes and inhale deeply.

3. Continue breathing deeply, hold, and slowly release each breath.

4. Visualize the air filling your lungs and then being expelled.

5. Now visualize a memory from your childhood. The first one that pops into your mind can be explored, but it's important to zero in on one at a time.

6. Try to pinpoint everything you can touch, hear, smell, see, and feel.

7. Ask yourself:

   A. Who is there with me?

   B. What are they doing?

   C. How is it making me feel?

8. Once you have your answers, end your session with some more deep breathing, and then open your eyes.

9. Use a journal to write down anything and everything you were able to gather from that memory.

10. Repeat as many times as needed. It's best to space sessions well, like once or twice a week, as revisiting traumatic events can take a toll on your mental health.

This step may seem simple but successfully performing your own guided imagery therapy takes time and continuous practice. Don't be too hard on yourself if you don't get it right on the first try, but don't give up. You can do this!

Dreamwork

Our subconscious minds often communicate with us through our dreams, unveiling buried emotions or emotions we're not even aware of. Have you ever had recurring dreams to the point where you can't stop pondering if there's more to them than meets the eye? I know I have. More often than not, our dreams reflect aspects of our character, perceptions, beliefs, and fears. This is why, when attempting to connect with your inner child, it helps to take time to **decipher** the meaning or cause behind certain dreams, as they may lead to explanations and a chance to lay important matters to rest. You could find that they relate to unresolved issues of the past or are sometimes memories of your childhood. Your inner child may be using dreams as a means to communicate with you and let you know that they need help moving past certain traumas.

Think back on any significant dreams or ones you couldn't help but remember that left you feeling unusually incomplete and not knowing why. Do any of them share similarities? This could have some deeper meaning than simple dreaming. Once you identify a possible message behind a dream, think back on your childhood. Any moment in those memories that resembles an emotion you're often haunted by should be considered one of the wounds that have shaped the adult you find yourself to be.

It might help to speak to a close relative, friend, or professional about your dreams, and what they mean to you, or what you think they mean. These individuals can help tremendously by offering their opinions, support, and even tips on alternative ways to interpret or embrace your dreams.

Signs of Trauma in Various Stages of Childhood

To know if certain memories mean anything or point to specific events of the past, you should recap what each stage of your childhood was like. Look for clues or signs that might help paint a clearer picture of events that **transpired** so that you can establish if any of them are somehow connected to your character and habits as an adult.

Preschool Phase

Try to remember if you had a habit of screaming or crying often. You can also think back on whether you frequently experienced nightmares as well as intense anxiety when separated from a parent or caregiver. Poor eating habits that caused significant weight loss or gain. While this period would've been an early start, for some individuals, this is true.

Elementary Phase

Look for patterns of sleeping problems or difficulty staying focused in school. You may also remember feeling perpetually anxious, fearful, or guilty. It can be hard to pinpoint specific events but just be sure to look for a trend of experiencing negative emotions.

Middle and High School Phase

Think about any behaviors that stand out to you now as an adult. Perhaps you had self-harming habits or you suffered from eating disorders. You might even have engaged in **detrimental** sexual habits and substance abuse like alcohol and recreational drugs. Pay attention to memories of constant loneliness and depression.

Common Types of Childhood Trauma

In many cases, we struggle to identify the trauma within ourselves and the events that created it. In part, this is because we've developed the habit of ignoring certain harsh truths about our childhoods, and in part, it is our literal inability to recognize that some events were in fact traumatic. We may not have a healthy basis to compare our experiences to, and as such, we remain blissfully unaware.

We're going to talk about some common types of childhood trauma so that you can finally have that basis and reflect on your experiences as a more informed person.

Assault

This can be a physical or sexual assault. It is not limited to one attack but is typically not experienced repeatedly. An assault victim has typically been exposed to a single attack that may leave them in a state of permanent **hyper-alertness**.

Refugee

Individuals with refugee-related trauma are those who've been exposed to war. Refugee children witness unspeakable atrocities that leave them with long-term physical and mental health issues. Their families are often subjected to torture and being first-hand witnesses is not uncommon.

Severe Grief

This refers to the abrupt loss of a loved one. It doesn't have to be as a result of death; it can be through the divorce of parents or separation from the caregiver. Traumatic grief can have much more serious complications than many of us are aware of and produce PTSD-like symptoms. Some effects of severe grief include intense anger, sadness, withdrawal, or difficulty concentrating. They may also struggle with feelings of guilt or abandonment long after their loss.

Neglect

Neglect happens when our caregivers fail to meet our basic needs like food, shelter, and love. It can lead to feelings of being invisible, unimportant, and unworthy of love and care. This lack of nurturing can also result in feelings of emptiness, low self-esteem, and difficulty forming healthy relationships. You might grow to be someone with trust issues, have trouble regulating emotions, and experience chronic feelings of loneliness and isolation.

Domestic Violence

Trauma as a result of domestic violence refers to abusive behavior between caregivers or within the family environment. This means the victim may experience or witness physical violence, verbal abuse, emotional manipulation, or other forms of mistreatment. The scars of this type of trauma run deep and can also cause lasting emotional, physical, and behavioral damage.

Bullying

This is quite an underestimated type of trauma and we often assume that as long as a child is no longer exposed to bullying, the effects of it will **dissipate**. However, the effects of bullying can trail you into adulthood through constant fear, sadness, and a deep sense of isolation. This emotional pain may result in severe anxiety, depression, and low self-esteem, which can make everyday interactions and academic performance more challenging.

Natural Disasters

The overwhelming sense of helplessness one feels when subjected to the trauma of a natural disaster is incomprehensible. Many times, you have symptoms of PTSD, like progressive anxiety, night terrors, and a perpetual fear that it can happen again. You might also notice that you have heightened stress responses and find extreme difficulty feeling safe.

Violence and Acts of Terrorism

These kinds of traumatic events refer to community violence, like violent protesting, looting, and rioting. Acts of terrorism refer to mass shootings, bombings, and attacks of this nature. Witnessing and enduring such horrific events can lead to confusion, intense fear, and **agoraphobia** (an anxiety disorder triggered by leaving home or familiar spaces). The anxiety caused by such events can become crippling if not addressed adequately and timely.

Race-Related Trauma or Xenophobia

Another form of trauma often under-discussed is the effects of race-related trauma like blatant racism or discrimination. The effects of **xenophobia** can be grouped into the same class as those of race-related trauma, as they both result in severe mistreatment of individuals of a different race or from a different country. Unfortunately, not many people discuss just how prominent this type of trauma still is and how it often leads to chronic stress, low self-esteem, and internalized negative beliefs about yourself and your cultural identity.

Exploitation

Here we're talking about the deliberate exploitation of a minor, whether it's sexual exploitation or labor-related. This is still a very real problem worldwide, as trafficking takes place in all parts of the world. Victims of this type of trauma experience extreme feelings of powerlessness, anxiety, and deep-seated fear. Somehow, victims of exploitation tend to feel guilty, as if they were the ones who did something wrong. They also commonly feel shame, which slowly progresses into chronic depression, trust issues, and feelings of worthlessness.

It's so important that you seek immediate help if you feel chronic, intense negative emotions, as you could be delaying an **inevitable** breakdown. Many victims of trauma who don't get the help they need tend to resort to substance abuse, violence against others, violence against themselves, or suicide. No victim deserves to be left to navigate the waters of recovery by themselves, as they have no idea what they're doing, where to begin, or where they're going. Everyone deserves support and guidance and these can only be provided if you are honest with yourself about the trauma that has defined you until this point and you take the first steps toward healing.

Impact of the Wounded Inner Child on Adulthood

Not every wounded inner child suffered the same extent of trauma, and not everyone carries that trauma in the same way. For instance, someone could have been given all the worldly possessions they could dream of, yet their emotional needs were neglected, and that resulted in a deep sense of insecurity in their adult relationships. A person like this might need constant reassurance in their romantic relationships, or perhaps they completely emotionally detach from everyone as a defense mechanism. The key is understanding how your childhood trauma affects your adulthood and finding ways to heal.

Case Study

Another case I handled involved Elijah, a man from a successful family. His father's strict expectations on how a man should behave, emphasizing anger as the only acceptable emotion, added pressure on Elijah. God forbid he was unhappy or saddened by something; he'd be berated endlessly until rage overshadowed all other emotions.

"What's so wrong with needing a hug and a "It's going to be okay, son," every once in a while?" He posed, opening up to me.

He **bawled** his eyes out, pleading to know what he could do to earn the right to be hurt. His father passed years before our paths crossed, yet his teachings lived on in Elijah. Every relationship he'd ever had failed miserably. Not only because vulnerability was perceived to be exclusively for women but also because talking about it would require acknowledging it to come with, and this was unacceptable; men got angry, not **sentimental**. Alone, confused, and overcome with emptiness, he took the first step toward healing. He revisited all the toughest memories of his father, and even though he wasn't around anymore, Elijah spoke to him and let him know just how free he was.

"I forgive you," he said, during a guided imagery session. "You didn't know any better, but I want you to know that I do. I've found strength in vulnerability, and it's made me the man I always knew I could be."

Our childhood experiences greatly influence our adult lives, impacting our behaviors, beliefs, and relationships. Unresolved childhood trauma can result in self-doubt, fear, and self-sabotaging habits that hinder growth and happiness. Thus, we need to understand the link between past traumas and current challenges, as it is vital for healing. By acknowledging how our inner child's wounds still affect us, we can start to break free from their hold.

Embrace the journey of healing your inner child as an act of self-love and bravery. It entails confronting your pain with compassion, nurturing your wounded inner self, and seeking forgiveness. As we embark on this healing path, we empower ourselves to rewrite our story, break away from the past's influence, and welcome a future of healing, growth, and resilience.

Chapter 2:

The First Steps to Healing

It can be said that many people are blissfully unaware of the damage caused by traumatic or emotion-fueled experiences from our past and their effects on our fundamental characteristics. It can also be said that some of us, who are fully aware of the magnitude of our own psychological brokenness, actively choose to ignore it. We're so afraid to be honest with ourselves and say, "Yes, I know this is what made me who I am." Our motives behind this denial or elective ignorance vary from person to person. Some fear that acknowledging it somehow gives it **dominion** over them, while others are simply not strong enough to keep it together when the ocean of emotions related to specific incidents comes flooding in.

This is the chapter where I'll demonstrate that avoidance is never the answer. Acceptance and acknowledgment are not signs of defeat, so don't allow your wounded inner child to be caged up. The last thing you want is to victimize your inner child any more than they already have been. Now is the time for you to realize that embracing your wounded inner child is the foundational step on the road to healing.

Embracing Acknowledgment and Acceptance

I need you to remain open-minded when it comes to this step. This might very well be one of the hardest steps, but it's crucial to recovery. There will always be a "logical" explanation for why you are the way you are, but nothing is as accurate and consistent as the concept of the inner child. Have you ever gotten so mad that you involuntarily resorted to child-like reactions like flinging a mug against the wall or screaming over the person you're in an argument with so you can't hear them? Well, to me, that sounds like an inner child briefly surfacing.

More often than not, a wave of extreme emotion washes over us before we **deduce** that our inner child is screaming for help, but we're so afraid to feel that pain with them that we bury it deep down and cling to odd behaviors, self-destruction, and other **peculiar** habits just to avoid dealing with it. We do our utmost to drown out their voices until eventually they're long forgotten, tucked away in our subconscious. Then one day, without warning, we have no choice but to address the elephant in the room.

My goal is to prevent the complete breakdown of the coping structure you have set up for yourself by helping you find healthy, constructive outlets. Outlets that will not only help you cope with your past trauma but slowly overcome it.

Let's brainstorm some ways that can help you get started with healing your wounded inner child.

Dig Deep

This might not be necessary for everyone, but it's especially necessary for those of us who've devoted our lives to placing our childhood traumas into an **impenetrable** container and clasping the lid on so tightly that not even we can tap into it at will. It may require speaking to older relatives who were around when you were younger, looking at old family photographs and videos, visiting familiar places, and so forth. You can also engage in activities that were common in your childhood, as it places you in a similar state of mind as back then, which can be essential to unlocking various aspects of what you felt in those moments as well as highlighting what you may have wished to feel instead. The key here is to fully immerse yourself in your own history so that the memories will just come flooding back.

Connect the Dots

Now that you know what, when, where, who, why, and how, it's time to start thinking about how those specific events impact your current life. What habits have arisen and stuck since that time? Can they truly be traced back to those moments? How does knowing about this make you feel now? This exercise is not to establish blame but rather to help you see just how significant that buried memory actually is to you. In order to ensure that you don't overload yourself and go into shock, you may want to try doing these activities in stages and keeping a journal or notebook for when you move on to the next stage. This will help you stay focused on specific events and emotions that you deem significant without having to try and remember them all yourself.

Meditate

The purpose of meditation is to bring your mind and body to complete relaxation and enable you to focus more clearly on certain moments. Tapping into various memories through meditation can help uncover and revisit the emotions experienced at that time. Not everyone can simply start meditating and immediately experience **revelation**, which is why there is something like guided meditation. Guided meditation is step-by-step instruction that seamlessly walks you through the process of achieving complete calmness and helps you know what to look for in your memories.

It's imperative that your newfound awareness isn't wasted, ignored, or neglected. You've now developed the ability to tap into the events that shaped you, which means you can now redefine their effects. Healing won't come easy and will take a lot of trial and error, but through consistency, you can do it.

You might be asking yourself, "How do I even begin the healing needed to redefine events that were so significant and have become a fundamental aspect of my core existence?" Well, let's discuss some of the ways that you can begin healing your wounded inner child.

Write a Letter

You know your inner child better than anyone, and after revisiting those events and emotions, you should have a solid grasp of what they are feeling. Writing a letter to them acknowledging their presence and the message they've long been trying to get through to you is a great way to start your communication with them. Let them know that their voice has finally been heard, and you will do whatever it takes to set them free. Convey your acceptance of their presence in your words and speak as honestly as you can. Remember, this is your inner child, whose anguish has been buried and often forgotten, so we owe it to them to truly **immerse** ourselves in their world and commit ourselves to nurturing their recovery as best we can. Allow them the freedom to experience their emotions fully without trying to stop or interrupt moments of vulnerability. For instance, if recalling traumatic events leads to overwhelming sadness, allow your inner child to weep, scream, or deal with the feeling in that moment exactly as they see fit without convincing yourself that there's no need to get emotional. Of course, there is. This is your road to recovery, and you should feel comfortable bursting into tears at any point during the process.

Regular Check-Ins

Checking in on your inner child is essential to avoid falling into the same habit of overlooking and dismissing them. Take time regularly to check in on them and really zero in on whether anything feels off. If something feels off, you might be experiencing triggers in your day-to-day life that you're not even aware of. Be patient and kind with them, as this healing is an ongoing **endeavor** and there are bound to be ups and downs. The key to successful check-ins is to have a proper dialogue with your inner child and identify any issues that may be lurking.

Identify Triggers

Healing can give you a new lease on life, but when the wounds run as deep as your inner child, it's impossible to escape all the triggers. You need to establish what your triggers are and work towards reducing as many of them as possible. For instance, certain smells, movies, people, places, and even foods can all trigger your inner child's trauma-related responses. Arguments with a romantic partner or witnessing the arguments of another couple can even spark the emotions linked to your wounded inner child. Minimizing your exposure to triggers will strengthen your connection with your inner child and can help give you a sense of control.

Listen With Intent

Your inner child might reach out to you at random times and you should always be prepared to listen. Not only to understand what they are feeling but also to help **alleviate** whatever is causing them distress.

This requires you to ask your inner child questions like (Johnson, 2022):

> *What exactly is it you're feeling?*
>
> *Are you judging yourself too harshly?*
>
> *Is there anything you're blaming yourself for and why?*
>
> *What can I do to support you?*

Knowing the answers to these questions can be the defining factor in determining whether you can properly heal or not.

Professional Assistance

For some reason, there's a negative stigma attached to professional help when it comes to mental care. It's also imperative to know that being able to do this by yourself is extremely hard and there's absolutely nothing wrong with seeking professional assistance. It can happen that you try everything humanly possible to heal on your own, but you just don't seem to get the results you're hoping for. This is when you need to speak to someone qualified to help you navigate these waters.

Keep in mind that a lot of the damage caused by these traumatic events has taken years to shape us and there are no overnight solutions to healing. Sometimes, we're also not knowledgeable or qualified enough to know where the problems truly lie or how to begin the recovery so professional guidance and insight are crucial. There are so many options available in these modern times; you don't even have to be in the same room as your mental health professional to get the assistance you need.

Professional mental health services can be delivered through

- in-person, outpatient sessions.

- online support.

- telephonic support.

- group sessions.

- mobile applications.

Creating Your Safe Healing Space

Healing can only take place in a space where you feel truly free and comfortable being open and vulnerable. This means the environment you're surrounded by needs to be **conducive** to healing or your attempts may be in vain. Be mindful of the fact that creating a space for healing refers to more than just your physical surroundings.

Let's unpack this statement a bit more, shall we?

So, first, let's start with the tangible aspects of your healing space:

- Should be clean, decluttered, and tailored to your preferences.

    ○ think of a tranquil setting with calming lights, relaxing aromas, etc.

- Should be easily accessible and uninterrupted.

    ○ preferably at home (to eliminate inconvenience that might ultimately lead to avoidance)

- Should immediately fill you with feelings of hope and strength.

    ○ decor or artwork that evokes happiness and empowerment (positive quotes, inspirational messages, photographs of happy memories)

Now, let's move on to the **intangible** aspects of your healing space:

- Avoid anyone or anything that negatively affects your mood before entering this space.

    ○ a bickering co-worker, a toxic family member, or a romantic partner.

- Set boundaries that protect your mental well-being and do not make any exceptions.

    ○ If you plan to dedicate an hour or even 15 minutes daily to working on your healing, do not allow anyone to change that.

○ Any triggers you've removed should also not be allowed back into your life, even briefly.

- Employ positive self-talk.

○ Listing five or more qualities you like about yourself before starting can help get you into the right mindset.

As long as your healing space allows you the freedom to truly reflect and rebuild, it is a success.

The Power of Self-Compassion

Self-compassion is often underrated, and I don't think we encourage it enough. People seem to minimize or completely dismiss the necessity of being kind to themselves. As adults, we're programmed to be the shoulder to cry on or the voice of comfort for those who need it, but when it comes to ourselves, we're completely intolerable to our mistakes, unwilling to accept anything less than perfection. Yes, you're good at many things, and yes, you could've done some things differently, but does that really mean that you deserve to be punished when you make a mistake?

Learning to be patient and compassionate with yourself will dramatically speed up your healing, whether you realize it or not. Harsh inner self-critics are typically a **manifestation** of learned behavior from our youth. If our parents and guardians **instill** the expectation of flawlessness, we tend to carry their ideals in our subconscious. This means that every time you do something you know will disappoint or upset them, your mind immediately creates an inner dialogue **chastising** your choices and competence. This toxic trait takes time to develop and is typically involuntary.

Perpetual intolerance for your own mistakes, as well as that of others is the outcome of continuous exposure to **castigation** and can be nearly impossible to weed out. Thankfully, with concerted effort and the active application of helpful programs and techniques, you can slowly reclaim your individuality and acceptance of yourself with all your imperfections.

How Self-Compassion Promotes Inner Healing

Self-compassion helps reduce anxiety, depression, and stress in general. Of course, nobody enjoys falling short of their own expectations of themselves or letting someone down, but the reality is that no one can do it all. We all face moments where we feel inept or fail to produce the results we set out, but self-compassion is the deciding factor in how well we handle those feelings.

Self-compassion allows you to embrace your failures and shortcomings with open arms, rather than wallow in self-pity and negative thoughts. Persistent negative thoughts increase stress, which is without a doubt disastrous for your physical and mental well-being. Perpetually high levels of stress can lead to an overproduction of *cortisol*. Cortisol is the primary stress-related hormone, and although its main function is to assist your body with handling stress, it goes without saying that excessive amounts would cause an array of unwanted and often unmanageable symptoms.

Here are some of the unpleasantries related to excess cortisol:

Psychological

- inability to concentrate

- mood swings

- depression

- insomnia

- mental fatigue

Physiological

- elevated blood pressure

- blemish breakouts

- brittle bones

- excessive weight gain (typically around the midsection, in the face, and on the upper back)

- elevated blood sugar

- weak muscles

- unusual and increased hair growth

- skin **depreciation** leading to easy bruising and slow healing

- chronic headaches

I think it's safe to say that whether you're experiencing one or all of these symptoms, it significantly impacts your daily life. Self-compassion has been shown to eliminate or reduce the effects of stress, as it helps you reframe the way you perceive setbacks and personal inadequacies. This is an essential skill, as it cultivates resilience and a growing mindset.

Self-Compassion Techniques

Recognizing and understanding the need for self-compassion is only one step in a life-long endeavor toward healing your wounded inner child. Let's discuss some techniques you can use right now to get you started on your self-compassion journey.

Mindfulness

Being mindful involves being completely aware of how you're feeling in the current space and time. It requires you to welcome every thought and emotion, accept them, and then release them. This fosters the habit of addressing your emotions as opposed to ignoring them. There are many ways to incorporate mindfulness into your everyday life, like yoga and meditation. We will be looking at a combination of mindfulness meditation and breathing exercises.

- Find a quiet, uninterrupted space.

- Sit on a comfortable pillow on the floor, or sit on a comfortable chair.

- Start by taking a deep breath in through the nose and then slowly releasing it through your mouth.

- Pay attention to the rise and fall of your chest as the air enters and exits your lungs.

- Now visualize the air filling your lungs and then escaping it.

- You can now zero in on what you are feeling. This can be achieved through introspection by asking yourself questions like:

    o *How is your day going?*

    o *Did anything happen to influence your emotions, whether good or bad?*

    o *How do you feel right this minute?*

- Once you've established how you feel, fully immerse yourself in that emotion. Remind yourself that what you're feeling is natural and nothing to be ashamed of.

- Continue controlling your breathing as you acknowledge your emotions, and exhale deeply as you allow yourself to let those emotions go.

- Visualize the weight of that experience or memory exiting your body.

- Finish off with a few more deep breaths as you welcome and embrace the possibility of new opportunities and new emotions.

This exercise can be done daily for about 10-15 minutes, but I know that not everyone has the time to do this as frequently as the next person, so try to have at least two sessions weekly. You should also aim for 10 minutes, as it can take a while to truly get into the right mindset.

Self-Compassion Meditations

Meditation can be done in various ways; some people lie down, some people sit on the floor in a private space, and some people need to be surrounded by nature. You need to be sure to select an option that you know will allow you to fully relax and open your mind.

Find a quiet, uninterrupted space. Now, sit down on a comfortable pillow on the floor or sit on a comfortable chair. Next, you're going to control your breathing to be intentional and calm. Begin to think or utter positive self-compassion affirmations.

Use the following to get you started:

I love who I am and who I am becoming.

There is no shame in making mistakes.

I will love myself even when I make mistakes.

I forgive myself for everything I've done wrong.

I deserve love and forgiveness.

It takes a strong person to accept themselves for who they are.

I am strong.

My mistakes are proof that I am learning and growing.

Others' opinions and judgments of me do not define me.

My flaws are not limitations but rather testaments to my individuality.

I am unique, and I don't need to be like anyone else.

Everyone feels the way I do, and it's completely natural.

I can be whoever I choose to be.

Failures are opportunities for growth.

How I feel about myself is more important than how others feel about me.

As long as I am happy and healthy, I can do anything.

You will be amazed to discover the healing power of speaking positively to yourself and how self-compassion will not only boost your self-confidence but also reframe how you perceive yourself and others. Be sure to allocate as much time for self-compassion meditation as you would for mindfulness exercises, because it forces you to make time to show yourself kindness. Sessions should be done daily, but twice or three times a week can also yield outstanding results. Feel free to incorporate the burning of incense or essential oils into your sessions. Anything that contributes to your calming atmosphere is a positive addition.

Remember that healing can't take place overnight, and everyone heals in different ways and at different rates, so be sure to avoid setting a timeframe for progress. As long as you remain consistent with your practices, you are on the right path, and healing is on the horizon!

Chapter 3:

Connecting With Your Inner Child

Once you've opened yourself to being vulnerable and embraced the presence of your wounded inner child, the rest of the steps become a little easier. Still, not knowing how or where to begin can significantly **impede** and often halt your healing. I want to be sure that you have all the tools you need to not only get started but to help keep you on the path of rebirth and recovery.

This is why our focus for this chapter is going to be different techniques and tips to help you connect with your inner child.

A Mirror to Your Soul

Have you noticed how looking in the mirror and liking what you see can sometimes feel impossible? Some people find that they can't even look at their own reflection without feeling shame or displeasure at the sight before them. Can you imagine how difficult and unbelievably heartbreaking that feeling must be? How does one despise their own reflection and how do we change this?

Well, the bad news is that you're likely not the reason why those negative opinions about yourself have been formed. It's more likely that you were subjected to harsh criticism in your youth, which left you with a **distorted** idea of what you should achieve or attain before you can consider yourself beautiful and worthy of acceptance and love. The good news is that you possess the power to completely reframe that perception and train yourself to love what you see in yourself, flaws and all.

Mirror work is your best friend in this situation. This requires you to not only look at your reflection but to genuinely gaze into the depths of your soul and unearth your true self. Once you've connected with your true self, you can then begin communicating. You're going to speak kindly and honestly in order to draw out your inner child. Your inner child desperately needs to feel acknowledged and as soon as that approval is provided, a foundation of trust is laid and rehabilitation can now commence.

Here's how you can begin your mirror work:

- Stand or sit in front of a mirror (it works best when your full body or at least full upper body is visible in the mirror).

- Take a deep breath, hold it in for five seconds, and then release.

- Now, begin your conversation. You can start by acknowledging the presence of your inner child with:

- o Hi, I know you're there, and I'm sorry for burying your voice for so long.

- o I'm ready to hear what you need to help set us free.

- Next, you want to address the issues you think led to your wounds. Try asking:

  - o Are you still hurting because of this? If yes, why?

  - o How did that event make you feel?

  - o What do you need to do to overcome the emotional damage caused by it?

- You can now offer comforting words to help your inner child accept that those events are in the past and unchangeable. Your words should also convey that you forgive them and that they should forgive themselves.

  - o It wasn't your fault.

  - o There is nothing wrong with feeling the way you do.

  - o Nobody is perfect, and that's okay.

  - o We deserve to be free from those wounds.

- End your session with the assurance that you will be there, doing whatever you need to continue moving forward.

  - o I matter.

  - o My happiness is my number-1 priority.

  - o My needs and wants matter.

- I will not remain a victim of my past traumas.

- I will never stop loving myself exactly the way I am.

At first, talking to yourself in the mirror can feel a bit strange; hell, you might even feel silly and embarrassed. The reason why mirror work needs to be verbal is because positive thoughts can only take you so far. There is a transformative atmosphere and aura that wash over you when you speak aloud to yourself. Therefore, verbalizing your acknowledgment of your own humanity will be one of the most powerful weapons in your arsenal.

The purpose of revisiting your childhood memories is not to assign blame but rather to understand the root cause behind your wounds and start healing from them. It helps to create a timeline of all significant events instead of singling out the negative ones alone. With compassion and curiosity, not judgment, we explore **pivotal** moments, unraveling patterns that shaped our beliefs and emotional responses. This exercise fosters self-understanding and healing, empowering us to rewrite our narrative with resilience and authenticity.

Journaling From the Heart

In many aspects of life, journaling has proven to be a therapeutic and creative outlet. While journaling may seem like a simple task, the objective is not only to write down your thoughts. The objective is to create written pieces that act as a conversation between you and your inner child. Your goal when journaling is to give your inner child a voice and hear the cries you've missed or ignored for so long.

Journaling not only encourages us to address our inner child, but it also ensures that we can be 100 percent honest about what we feel and think. When you take the time to **introspect** and peel away all the layers of adopted personality and defenses you've spent years cultivating, you already offer your inner child a sense of safety. This safety is vital to the healing process because your inner child can only guide you if it trusts that you will do what is best for them when you reach your destination.

Here are some prompts designed to draw out your inner child and let them know that this is the beginning of their liberation.

What were your hopes for your future?

What were you afraid of?

Who were you closest with?

Do you have trust issues?

What do you fear others will discover about you?

Which teachers and subjects did you like?

Did you have a role model as a child? Who was it?

Why did you look up to them?

Is your life now what you always hoped it would be?

Who were your best friends, and why?

Tell me about an experience where you were overwhelmed with fear. How did you handle that situation?

What made you happy as a child?

Tell me about the first time you felt betrayed or hurt.

How do you deal with uncomfortable emotions?

Do you have a first memory? What is it?

Did you ever blame anyone for making you feel unpleasant emotions? Who were they, and why did you blame them?

Which traits from your childhood remained with you into adulthood?

What is your biggest fear right now?

Do you feel envious or jealous of anyone?

Is there anyone you have a grudge against, and why? What can be done to help you let go of these grudges?

Do you ever feel anxious? Why? How do you handle those feelings?

Has anyone made you feel ashamed? How can you let go of such emotions?

Tell me about a happy time. Who was there, and how did you feel?

Are there any other times now that make you feel that level of happiness?

If not, how can you create moments that will?

Who was your inspiration, and why?

Who is your inspiration now?

Are you being kind enough to yourself? How can you be kinder and more self-loving?

What do you love about yourself?

Name three things you are proud of yourself for.

What makes you nervous now? Is it the same as when you were a child? How can you manage these emotions?

Are there any emotions you actively avoid?

What are your current dreams for your future?

Do you owe anyone from your childhood an apology? If yes, you could write them a letter, call them, or reach out to them on social media.

What does it mean to forgive, and how can you show yourself forgiveness?

These questions often give rise to more questions and that is the beauty of this exercise. It's only the first step in a lifelong dialogue with your inner child. You will be able to bury old grudges you may not even have known you still kept or discover ways to better manage your emotions. Everything your inner child so sorely needs can be established through this exercise.

Daily Diary

As old-fashioned as this may seem, you'll find that keeping a daily diary is like having a friend alongside you through all your ups and downs. You are forced to pay attention not only to the negative occurrences of the day but also to the positives as you gradually program yourself to store details about your day that you'll share with your diary.

Daily diaries are also useful to re-read when you take time to reflect on and review your progress. You notice trends in your day, those you surround yourself with, and your general environment. You can easily pick up on areas that require less attention and areas that require more attention since you're able to view the happenings of your day from an outside lens or perspective.

Keeping a daily diary is also just a great way to have a friend that you share absolutely everything with, as we often fear that our actual loved ones and friends might judge us for some of the things we feel, say, and do.

Reconnect With Childhood Friends

Technology and the internet are wonderful things, aren't they? We have a **plethora** of devices and applications we can use to locate and get in touch with people we grew up with. Don't be afraid to look up the friends you had as a child, catch up on old times, and **reminisce** about the past. Sometimes seeing these individuals offers a great deal of **nostalgia** that can be used to unearth memories and emotions from the past. So, next time you get an invitation to attend a reunion, jump at it! You never know what amazing avenues lie ahead.

Responsible Rage Release

From a young age, we've been taught that anger and rage are negative and should never be allowed to control our actions. However, continuous repression can result in a complete meltdown eventually or outbursts in other toxic ways. So, in the spirit of evoking a reaction from your inner child and bringing their issues to the surface, why not release that rage in a controlled environment? Throw ice cubes on the ground outdoors, break plates, hammer old broken furniture, or wrestle a pillow or giant stuffed animal. There's no harm in getting that rage out of your system and allowing your inner child to experience that release too is an added bonus.

Connect With Children

What better way to connect with your inner child than to spend time around children? Discover new ways to enjoy being a child and be playful. Children offer some of the simplest solutions for having fun and letting go of the seriousness that comes with being an adult. Sometimes even simple conversations with children open your mind to what you've been missing and offer ways to incorporate that innocent fun into your busy life. You may be reminded of some of the things you liked to do as a child and can even share them with the children around you so you have the joy of knowing you've left a piece of yourself and your inner child with them.

Creative Pathways

Aside from the exercises mentioned above, there are various other ways you can connect with your inner child and begin the healing process. Some of us may not find it as easy to start off with affirmations or journaling and require introductory exercises before moving on to the above. So, this section is for anyone looking for alternative activities to incorporate into their connection regimen.

Creative expression is a powerful tool and highly recommended for nearly any form of therapeutic activity, as creativity bypasses our logical brain and speaks directly to our inner child. This is a spectacular method to employ since the hard part is taken care of by the chosen activity rather than you actively speaking to your inner child.

Let's explore some creative pathways known for their healing power.

Art Attack

We've become conditioned to believe that anything that someone can do professionally should only be pursued if you're absolutely fantastic at it. This notion is not only inaccurate; it also robs us of the freedom to indulge in the purest forms of self-expression. Stop overthinking these activities. You don't have to be the future Van Gogh to benefit from the **curative** powers of exploring your artistic side.

Another thing you should remember is that *art* isn't confined to paintings. There are so many different elements to art, like drawing, coloring, sculpting, and more. You should select the ones that resonate with you and if that means giving each one a try, then so be it!

Jam and Jive

Host a private dance party or get your kids involved. Music and dance have long been believed to improve mood and influence our emotions. It is also connected to better physical health, but let's discuss some of the most well-known benefits of this activity.

Here are the benefits that are supported by research (Cherry, n.d.):

- reduced appetite (depending on the tempo)

- pain management

- improved cognitive function

- improved memory

- stress reduction

- reduced depression

- increased motivation

- better sleeping habits

- better physical endurance

A Hug a Day Keeps the Inner Child at Bay

Yep, you heard me: hug it out! As basic as this activity appears to be, its effects will leave you **dumbfounded**. All healing doesn't have to be done through verbal **manifestations**. The power of touch is often underestimated and hugging yourself not only soothes your inner child but also promotes further exploration of self-love.

Below is an activity recommended by Traci Pedersen and Jamie Smith from Psych Central (n.d.):

Butterfly Hug

1. Place your hands on your chest.

2. Cross them over each other.

3. Connect your thumbs the way you would to create a hand butterfly.

4. Ensure your fingertips are just below your collarbones.

5. Begin to slowly tap your chest with one hand at a time.

6. You can now breathe in slowly and observe yourself becoming calmer.

7. Visualize your emotions and thoughts as you do a full emotional scan.

8. Release any judgments or harsh criticisms that automatically pop into your mind.

Involve Messy-Play

Messy-play refers to activities we loved as kids, like playing with slime, play-dough, finger painting, coloring, tie-dying clothing items, and so on. You can create marvelous works of art once you unleash the child in you and allow yourself the freedom to get down and dirty. Remember that this activity is for your personal enjoyment and there's no criteria for that, right?

It's natural to be skeptical about the efficacy of these activities, but they've been shown to work on more occasions than I can count. This is why psychologists and therapists recommend many of these in their programs, as they have proven to be highly beneficial. Though there's no one-size-fits-all with these activities, there is something for everyone.

All you have to do is understand and appreciate the fact that these exercises need to be performed in a fashion that is completely devoid of judgment and a hunger for instant results. This journey is one of continuous learning, growth, and healing, so expecting instant results is unreasonable.

Chapter 4:

Healing Through Re-Parenting

Healing requires much more work than activities and exercises that promote positivity. Through re-parenting, you can slowly undo or lessen the impact of childhood wounds. The concept of re-parenting is one that's not very well known. Let's start at the very beginning. Parenting is the act of rearing children. It **encompasses** more than providing financial stability.

Parenting entails providing physical and emotional security, teaching emotional regulation, encouraging learning and development through mistakes, and promoting a growth mindset. It also means offering unconditional love, nurturing self-confidence, and teaching effective communication skills. Now, when these values and skills are not taught in childhood, unfortunately, the damage becomes a permanent part of who we are, hidden in the depths of our subconscious in the form of our wounded inner child. This is what re-parenting aims to correct.

Re-parenting is the reintroduction of these essentials that should've been taught in childhood and slowly fosters the skills needed to be healthy, happy adults, undoing the damage done by the lack of parenting during childhood.

Negative Self-Image as a Result of Trauma

First, you need to recognize the trauma in yourself and establish exactly how it affects your perception of yourself and others. Doing so helps you understand that those perceptions are not only the results of wounds left by others, but they also highlight the possibility of change and hope.

Recognizing even the most subtle signs of damaged self-esteem is crucial for understanding and addressing this **pervasive** issue. These signs are not limited to specifics; however, more common ones are severe unhappiness with how you look, an **incessant** need to be liked or have all eyes on you, and an inability to positively handle criticism. You'll also notice that you don't make friends easily or that you don't feel as connected to friends as they do to you. That said, allowing yourself the time to genuinely reflect on your negative behaviors and thoughts opens the door to change, as you can now bring long-hidden signs of low self-esteem to the light.

Now that you know which signs to look for, it helps to seek out the underlying causes behind them. What is the reason why you have a negative self-image? Well, there are countless factors that influence our perceptions of ourselves, but the most influential factor is trauma. Discrimination, mental health problems, bullying, neglect, financial problems, and issues with your physical health can all lead to negative perceptions of yourself. These realities can lead to ruminating thoughts, which, in turn, may lead to dismissing caring for ourselves as best we can. It's often that we don't believe that we deserve to be cared for and that we ignore our basic needs for affection, self-love, good personal hygiene, and more. Then, looking into the mirror, we hate what we see, and we spiral out of control from there. Some people live in denial, portraying positive self-esteem as well as confidence in themselves, yet they are screaming on the inside. You need to understand that you are not the first one to feel this way, nor will you be the last, but the power to change how you perceive yourself is 100% in your hands.

Building Positive Self-Esteem

Improving self-esteem in adults with wounded inner children requires a **multifaceted** approach, beginning with the understanding that self-esteem is not a perception of ourselves. Instead, it varies over time; some days you're having a good self-esteem day, and other days you're not. This is completely normal.

In order to train yourself to improve your self-esteem, you need to cultivate self-awareness and engage in self-care practices. This requires you to recognize and steer clear of activities or situations that promote damage to self-esteem, such as comparing yourself to people you see on social media. It can also include the use or overuse of negative dietary supplements. Rather, devote your time and effort to doing things you enjoy. Reading for pleasure is a great way to substitute the toxic habit of obsessing over social media stars and what they have and don't have. You can learn new skills, like learning a new language or learning to paint. Get active, like hiking or even going for simple walks in the park. These activities are not just terrific **cognitive stimulation**; they also foster positive self-esteem as you are able to see just how capable you are.

Additionally, be sure to reach out to family and friends for advice and guidance. It's important that you know that everyone's trauma and healing journey is unique. Don't fall into the trap of comparing yourself and the rate at which you are healing with that of others.

The Foundation of Self-Care

Re-parenting is a powerful act of self-care and self-love that allows you to address the unmet needs from your childhood. By recognizing what you lacked in your upbringing, you can now provide yourself with the nurturing and care you once yearned for.

This may involve establishing consistent routines, embracing healthy nutrition habits, and granting yourself the freedom to play and rest without guilt. These simple yet profound acts of self-care are ways to nurture the inner child within us, fostering a sense of safety, comfort, and love. Healing from childhood wounds requires acknowledging past traumas and actively engaging in self-compassion and self-soothing activities. Through re-parenting practices, you can create a new narrative of kindness and understanding towards yourself, paving the way for emotional healing and growth. In essence, self-care becomes a transformative tool in the journey towards healing and self-discovery.

As difficult as it is to recognize the importance of self-care, you should force yourself to begin a routine and remain steadfast. If your inner child feels guilty for prioritizing themselves over others, you might be riddled with feelings of guilt, shame, and **inadequacy** since you've been conditioned to believe that the needs of others should take **precedence** over those of your own. Using self-care as the foundation for your re-parenting ensures that you truly understand the saying, "You cannot pour from an empty cup."

Surely, if you have children or plan on having children, you want to give them the best possible care and offer them the support you wish you had. Caring for yourself is essential to adopting the parenting skills needed to nurture and cultivate self-confidence, a willingness to learn, constructive communication, and overall resilience.

Identify What You Lacked

Before you can know which areas to focus on, you need to first establish which areas you did not receive proper parenting. Perhaps your parents never allowed you to be a kid and just play, so now as an adult, every time you take breaks to relax and unwind, you feel unproductive, and as such, you feel ashamed of your actions. Adults who were subjected to this type of parenting, or lack thereof, often feel inefficient when they are not working. They typically measure their worth by their work ethic.

Don't get me wrong, there's no harm in wanting to be successful and having a good work ethic; however, this should not define you nor should it be the determining factor in whether you deserve love and appreciation. So, this is an example of what to look for when identifying areas for re-parenting. Once you've determined what you need to work on, you can commence your re-parenting activities.

Conversations With the Child Within

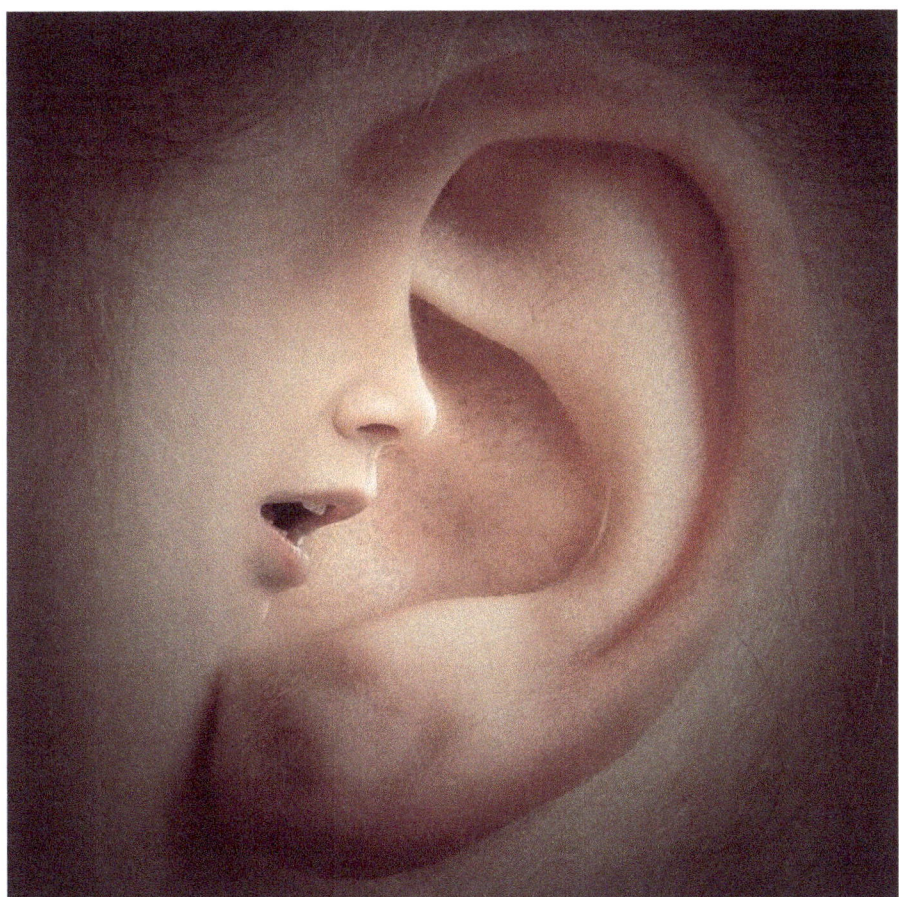

As we've covered in this book previously, the conversation you have with your inner child is crucial to building that connection. You can do so through journaling or even writing a letter. Remember to address your inner child directly, so instead of using your actual name, you may try using a nickname you used to have or a pet name that only those close to you use.

Be careful with your choice of words, as you are trying to undo the damage caused by harsh criticism and, in some cases, verbal abuse. Discuss every single thing that weighs heavy on your heart and mind without the fear of being **reprimanded** for bringing your family's shame or secrets to the surface. Many people struggle to even put in writing the difficult experiences that traumatized them because they're terrified of the effects dealing with those emotions again will have on them. Know that you can handle anything; consider the action you've taken with this book as the first of many courageous acts on your way to healing.

Here is an example of what a letter to your inner child might look like:

Dearest Nelly

I can't tell you how long I've waited to gain the courage to speak with you.

Do you remember that night when we were out with Mark and Ellie? It was right after their first son, Elliot, was born. Mark couldn't care less about helping Ellie, and she was struggling so much. I can still hear the cries she let out in the bathroom as I passed by. Not only did I feel your presence, but I also heard you screaming, "Help her!"

I guess it's because dad never helped mom with anything, and she always looked so tired. She would retreat to their bedroom every night with a look of sheer defeat painted on her face and the overwhelming sensation of alleviating her pain, gnawing at us. Every time I witness such selfishness, I feel your rage and try to hide it as best I can.

I now know why we get so mad when we see these things in others—it's because of what mom did to free herself from her misery. I remember you vowing never to drive your wife to self-harm and promising to be there 24/7, 365. Come hell or high water. I've discovered that this is why you're addicted to helping everyone, even when it's you who needs help sometimes.

I want you to know that there's nothing wrong with being the one who needs help sometimes. You do everything you can for everyone else, but you never allow anyone to know what you need. Taking care of yourself first is the most important part of taking care of others.

Let this be the beginning of me taking care of you. You deserve the help and love you so eagerly hand out to others. I promise this is the last time you have to feel this weight on your shoulders alone.

Together, we will become reborn.

The letters you write don't have to be limited to your inner child. It can be extremely helpful to write to anyone who's had a significant impact on the development of your inner child—a teacher, a family member, a fellow student, a friend, or even a stranger. Of course, it can also help to address a letter to the parent of your choice.

More often than not, releasing the anger and **animosity** we feel for our parents can be achieved by writing them a letter. You can tell them how they made you feel, the results of their parenting, and most importantly, that you forgive them. Know that forgiveness is not for the other person but rather for yourself. When you forgive them, you break free from the hold that **condemnation** had on you. This act of forgiveness has a ripple effect, as you will then be able to forgive yourself for the mistakes you've made as a result of that rage and misguided perception.

Re-Parenting Through Psychotherapy

For some, self-reparenting is easier said than done. Don't beat yourself up about it, and definitely don't give up. There are various services offered by mental health professionals that can be explored. If you realize that you need a bit more help with this, know that there is no shame at all in seeking assistance. You deserve to heal from these wounds, and the services provided by these professionals were designed for people just like you.

Psychotherapists often utilize the following forms of re-parenting (Davis, 2020):

Self-Reparenting

It empowers you to confirm positive self-aspects, promoting self-love and self-care without replacing the parent's ego state.

Spot Reparenting

It focuses on specific traumas and incidences and is developed for targeted trauma treatment.

Time-Limited Regression

Utilized for **schizophrenia** patients, intense structured nurturing is offered in five sessions.

Total Regression

It necessitates that you live with the therapist for extended care to change your parent's ego state.

It goes without saying that some of these will not be applicable to you. Your healthcare professional will first conduct an assessment or evaluation of sorts and ascertain exactly what you need to make this healing possible for you.

Boundaries as an Act of Love

Boundaries frequently get a bad rep because many people, generally those who have no respect for the boundaries of others, paint them in a negative light. People sometimes get upset, even offended, when you inform them of your boundaries, which tends to make you feel guilty for having them to begin with. These are typically the kinds of people who will test your boundaries or shame you for not allowing them to cross them. I'm here to tell you that you don't owe these people anything.

You don't owe it to them to be flexible with your boundaries, nor do you owe it to them to explain your boundaries. Anyone who truly cares about you and respects you will have no issue respecting your wishes. If that means adhering to even the simplest request for your peace of mind, then so be it.

What Exactly Are Boundaries?

So, do you think you know what boundaries actually mean? Well, I can tell you with certainty that this concept has proven to be something in somewhat of a gray area. Some people assume it's your principles, while others reckon it's personal rules you set for yourself and others to adhere to.

Boundaries are general preferences for all things related to yourself: interactions with you, your property, or anything that can be associated with you. They are typically developed during childhood and are often learned and adopted by those around you, but there are also those that simply manifest within you and you alone. Boundaries provide you with feelings of comfort, safety, ease, and respect, and when someone crosses your boundaries, it leaves you in a state of physical, emotional, or mental distress. This is why protecting your boundaries is so important. Your boundaries are there to protect you, but they cannot do that if you allow others to repeatedly disregard or disrespect them.

Though a certain level of flexibility is recommended, it's imperative that you don't make a habit of it. It's also imperative that your boundaries are healthy and not harmful to your well-being. Healthy boundaries produce happy and confident adults who feel content with their lives and their decisions and have immense self-control.

Different Types of Boundaries

Boundaries come in different forms. Have a look at the below to learn about the various types of boundaries there are:

Diffuse or Open Boundaries

These boundaries change frequently or apply only to some people. It's often a result of codependency and fosters that type of relationship.

Clear Boundaries

They are set openly and firmly. While there is room for exceptions (which generally need to be discussed first), there is mutual respect and acceptance of these boundaries, which fosters positive assertiveness.

Rigid Boundaries

These are boundaries that change for nothing and no one, regardless of the situation. Inflexibility is an understatement here, and these types of boundaries often foster isolation, impatience, and intolerance.

Next, we move on to some examples of boundaries.

Mental Boundaries

These boundaries refer to the thoughts and beliefs you hold. You set these boundaries because you know what you believe and deserve to be allowed the right to believe in what you want without someone perpetually trying to change it.

Knowing When It's Crossed

You will know when someone crosses your boundaries because you'll have a general sense of uneasiness or distress come over you to help you single out the signs and look for any form of language that ridicules your beliefs or thoughts. People often resort to minimizing, dismissing, or abating your beliefs too. These are all clear signs of crossing your boundaries.

Physical Boundaries

These can refer to any form of physical contact you will or will not allow with others. Of course, everyone won't have the same boundary applied to them. For instance, a family member might get a hug, whereas a colleague will get a handshake. These are perfectly acceptable, and you should never feel guilty about having them.

Knowing When It's Crossed

Look for any form of spoken or unspoken pressure that suggests they want more contact than you're willing to give. Often, you are also subjected to **beratement**. Another powerful and frequently successful tactic is playing the victim or acting offended by your boundaries. This is simply a means of manipulation and you shouldn't let it get to you. I think the worst of these is when they outright ignore your boundaries and just assume that you're going to tolerate their behavior, no questions asked.

Financial Boundaries

This, in essence, refers to the boundaries you set regarding spending habits. You might have a budget you'd like to stick to when it comes to how much you spend on living expenses and leisure and you might find yourself having to defend these boundaries more often than you think.

Knowing When It's Crossed

This often involves being coerced into spending more money than you want to or being shamed or called names until you succumb. Another trend here is to spend on your behalf, which, in turn, leaves you feeling even worse because you obviously don't want someone else to have to give out excessive amounts of money for you. You can also expect to be guilted into changing your mind.

Emotional Boundaries

Here, we're talking about anything you set as a way to protect your emotional well-being. Perhaps you don't like having public disagreements, so you set a boundary where any issues you and your partner have should be discussed in private.

Knowing When It's Crossed

You will notice a habit of minimizing the seriousness of your emotions or the complete dismissal of them. In some cases, they are less direct and are delivered in the form of jokes that embarrass you. When you confront them, they have no idea what you're talking about and make you feel as though you're imagining things. They might also resort to name-calling, often disguised as a joke or playful teasing.

There are many other elements to boundaries, like sexual and time boundaries, that are just as important. The message here is to take the time and really think about what your boundaries are. Write them down if you have to, and group them into ones that can be altered (when needed) and ones that are non-negotiable. Be sure to share them with absolutely everyone you interact with, as you cannot expect people to respect boundaries that haven't clearly been laid out for them. This doesn't mean you need to do it abruptly or **crudely**; inform them calmly and kindly about what it is you need them to know about you and how failure to do so will affect you and, in turn, affect them.

Setting Healthy Boundaries

Boundaries are like stop signs in your life, defined by your beliefs, values, culture, and family traditions. When setting them, consider your goals, start small, be clear, practice, and keep it simple.

Consider the following when setting boundaries:

- **Intention:** What is the goal of this specific boundary?

- **Starting point:** Which small area of my life can I start with? (Gradually move up to more significant ones.)

- **Clear explanation:** In order to hold someone accountable, you need to give them clear direction.

- **Preparation:** Properly prepare for the discussion. Write what you want to say down and set aside time afterward for questions.

- **Easily understandable:** Keep it short and sweet. Don't go too far into detail, or you may not get the actual message across.

Feeling guilty or vulnerable is normal when setting boundaries. To effectively cope with these feelings, it is crucial to first acknowledge and embrace the feelings of vulnerability or anxiety without trying to suppress or ignore them. Rather than **rationalizing** these emotions, listen to your inner child to grasp the underlying beliefs you have internalized. Reflect on your typical responses in such scenarios and observe how you have adjusted to protect yourself. Show appreciation for the part of yourself that has been safeguarding you, whether it appears as an overreaction or excessive accommodation. When someone violates your boundaries, any emotional discomfort should be regarded as a breach. It is then your responsibility to inform that person of how they made you feel and make sure they know you will not tolerate it.

You owe it to yourself to be comfortable with every situation you find yourself in and those you trust should be the last people allowed to disrupt that. Remind yourself that this is self-love in its purest form.

Toxic Myths You Should Be Aware Of

Now, it's also not uncommon for you to find yourself in situations where you're accused of outrageous things when setting boundaries. This is because there's a shared notion going around that if we love someone, we should be willing to put our own well-being and happiness aside for their sake. Don't get me wrong, we're always willing to make certain sacrifices for the ones we love, but there's a fine line between sacrificing something you can live without or don't necessarily need and **martyring** yourself because the other person won't understand. The ones who love us generally have no issue with taking a step back when we stand by our boundaries, but ever so often, they also try to manipulate you into allowing your boundaries to be crossed.

Below are some of the harmful myths you should be aware of should you ever have someone make these claims.

It's Rude

There are so many people being accused of being rude when they've set a boundary and refuse to budge. Individuals often use a guilt-trip strategy to get you to believe that you're being horrible for not allowing yourself to do something you don't want to. This is what is known as a "boundary-bully," and they specialize in prioritizing their own wants (Virro, 2020, p. 12). No matter how uncomfortable or even unhappy it makes you, they are perfectly content watching you allow them to dismiss your personal boundaries just to give them what they want.

If You Love Them, the Boundary Shouldn't Apply to Them

It's common for certain individuals to think that if someone loves them, there should be no boundaries between them and that boundaries are reserved for people outside the relationship. Some people even believe that this is the definition of a happy, healthy, and solid relationship. Unfortunately, this is regarded as a codependent relationship, and it's considered unhealthy for both individuals. Not knowing where your own values, opinions, and uniqueness begin means you've lost your individuality, and, in many cases, the things that once drew you to each other completely vanish.

Boundaries Are All About Saying No

This is especially the case with people who lacked boundaries in the past and are starting their journey to set some. They forget the purpose behind the concept and think that if they say no to everything, they will be protected from those who want to take advantage of them. Boundaries are not there as an indication that you think someone wants to take advantage of you but rather as a guideline for all those whom you interact with. It's a clear understanding you provide them regarding what you're willing to accept and do and what you're not.

It's Selfish

You'll often hear that your boundaries are a poor reflection of your character and suggest that you're selfish. Even if the person making this claim truly believes that this is selfish, they have a distorted perception of what it means to set boundaries. Perhaps they also have issues setting boundaries and are likely people-pleasers. In cases where the person knows the importance and value of boundaries but still pushes you to bend your own by accusing you of thinking only of yourself, just remember that not only are they wrong, but you might have to re-evaluate this person's presence in your life.

You're Pushing People Away

Communicating what you need to be the absolute best version of yourself shouldn't drive anyone away. If anything, it should bring people closer and strengthen connections because you are offering them open and honest communication. Rather than complain about them behind their backs, secretly loathe them, or completely go crazy on them when you've had enough, you inform them of the consequences of certain things well beforehand.

Remember that even with all the patience and explanations in the world, there will always be those who try to push your boundaries in order to see what they can get right with you; it's your job to stick to your guns. The more you reinforce them, the clearer you make it to the people that your boundaries will not be crossed.

And that's it for this chapter on healing through re-parenting. I want you to keep in mind that there is no exact science behind these methods nor is there a way for you to continually measure your progress. The only thing I can leave you with is the knowledge that these methods have worked for thousands of people and they're all healing at a pace that's tailored to them and their needs. There's no way to know how long it'll take before you're fully restored, but rather 10 steps every few months rather than no steps at all.

Chapter 5:

Overcoming the Hurdles

So, we've successfully begun our road to healing, and for some reason, like many others before us, we expect the road to be smooth sailing from here on out. Unfortunately, like many other aspects of life, healing from childhood wounds is not at all a seamless and obstacle-free road. There may come times when you think you've overcome certain challenges entirely, only to be triggered by an unexpected event and end up five steps back. Please understand that this is totally normal and that everyone experiences lapses in their abilities to remain strong.

Setbacks are nothing to feel ashamed of nor should they be given the power to halt or demolish the progress you've made. In this chapter, I'd like to help you realize the importance and value of hurdles as well as how to overcome them, rather than spend your journey toward healing fearing them, or trying to avoid them.

Facing Your Fears

In this crucial chapter about overcoming obstacles in the process of healing your wounded inner child, it's essential that you understand how to face and conquer the fears that arise. First, we must recognize the specific fears linked to our healing journey. These fears may appear as a resistance to being vulnerable or a hesitance to confront painful memories from our past. In order to identify these fears, you need to explore your emotions through introspection. We've discussed various ways to conduct introspections, so of course the method you select is one that is tailored to your needs.

Here's how you can get started with embracing your fears (Tabac, 2023):

Divulge the Origins

Think back to where this fear may have been born and what exactly caused it to stick. You might have to think back to each year of your childhood and mentally scan through the most significant memories of that time.

Relive the Emotions

In order to truly appreciate its influence, you have to allow yourself to experience every single emotion you felt at that time. It can be quite taxing, and sometimes, revisiting these memories opens a gateway for unexpected and long-forgotten emotions to resurface.

Reach Out to Your Inner Child

Help them acknowledge those emotions and let them know you are right there with them. They are not alone this time. Regression is a very real risk when attempting to unlock trauma and wounds from the past, but as long as you offer yourself and your inner child the reassurance and support you need to keep going, you'll get through it.

Provide Reassurance

Reassure your inner child that you know what they are feeling and that you are there to support them. You will be employing helpful techniques to work through your fears. Calm your wounded inner child by conversing with them about the strategies available to you for continued healing and recovery.

Refashion Your Perception

Find new ways to perceive those experiences. If you've learned anything from those moments, now is the time to list them. Think about any positives that come from those experiences and emotions.

Why Facing Our Fears Helps

You might wonder why everything leads back to revisiting unpleasant memories that you'd much rather not unravel, but you need to keep in mind that reflecting on our fears allows us to discover the underlying reasons for our anxieties. Well, the short answer is that the part of our brain, the **amygdala**, that is activated when we experience different emotions, releases cortisol and adrenaline so our bodies are prepared to react swiftly in order to protect us. This is true even if we're not in immediate danger. Anything our brains perceive as a threat is processed that way and this chemical reaction occurs.

Now, when we revisit painful memories, it's almost impossible to avoid those feelings of anxiousness and intense fear. So, naturally, the amygdala reacts in the same way that it would if we were in an actual threatening situation and releases those hormones. Perpetually being in a heightened state of alert (fight-flight-freeze state) eventually results in significant mental health complications. And we all know that mental well-being is essential to living a happy and healthy life, as well as making smart choices. This is why facing our fears is yet another pivotal part of healing.

Once these fears are identified, the next step is to develop personalized strategies to confront them. It's important to approach this process with kindness and understanding, understanding that healing requires time and dedication. One effective approach is to gradually expose yourself to challenging emotions or situations that trigger fear. For example, if you fear being vulnerable, you can try sharing deep feelings with someone close to you or even your mental health professional in a safe setting. Gradual exposure to vulnerability in small steps makes it easier to adapt to the discomfort of it and builds resilience over time.

The same can be done for those struggling with revisiting painful memories. Slow and steady really do win the race, so gradual exposure to those memories will surely make a notable difference in their effects on your emotional state. Start by revisiting less distressing memories and slowly progress to more difficult ones as you become more capable of coping.

Acknowledge Small Progressions

It's essential to acknowledge and celebrate even the smallest achievements and positive outcomes throughout this process. Each advancement toward facing fears demonstrates strength and resilience. By recognizing and internalizing these accomplishments, you cultivate a sense of empowerment and enhance your confidence in handling future challenges.

The Role of Resistance in Healing

You might think that once you've decided to take the steps toward healing, you'll embrace every aspect of it with open arms. We often forget that there are an array of things that could result in reluctance or resistance and these reactions will hinder our progress.

I want you to know that resistance is not just common; it's expected. It can take various forms, such as denial, procrastination, or a general discomfort with the changes that are unfolding. This is why you should be mentally prepared for such hurdles so that you are not the cause of your own defeat. You will need to learn to recognize the signs and understand the underlying causes behind such resistance before you can take the steps needed to overcome them.

Am I Resisting Healing?

I'm sure it seems a bit strange that I'm telling you to expect that you will resist your own healing. You might be thinking, "If I didn't want healing, then why would I have started in the first place?" But that's just it.

The resistance you experience is not necessarily linked to the overall goal of your healing journey; it may be certain aspects of the process that cause you so much discomfort that you would rather drop everything than persevere. I've seen so many people show up for their healing exercises for more than five sessions and then just quit. It seems sudden to an outsider, but to the person experiencing those issues, it feels like a long time coming.

They might even wonder if they're doing something wrong or if something is fundamentally wrong with them because the activities are simply not working for them. Some people even admit that they don't see anything during the visualization exercises. Now, before we continue, let's just unpack this part. There is absolutely nothing wrong with any of you if you don't encounter the same results or effects as the next person. Each one of us is a unique individual and absorbs information and experiences in different ways so we cannot measure our progress against someone else's. You will never reach your own destination if you're trying to follow another person's path.

The reality is that in many of these cases where you feel **stagnant** and you just don't feel the process working, it's the product of still not having gained full control over your ability to reshape your life. Your subconscious still feels trapped by the will of whoever instilled these insecurities and fears in you, so you are struggling to grasp the magnitude of your own strength.

In other cases, you might be in too much control so your subconscious is incapable of temporarily handing the wheel over to the person guiding you on your healing journey. Your inner child may have decided a long time ago that never again will anyone control them, and as such, not even the instructions set out for the sake of their healing can get them to follow along. It's essential that you identify which is the case for you, as you need to know what's causing this resistance before you can deal with it.

Tips for Challenging Your Resistant Inner Child

As soon as you've done some soul-searching and discovered that your inner child is going to be a bit harder to bring over to the enlightened side, you may have to resort to some tough love techniques.

Here are some things you can try:

- **Reason with them:** This is the most favorable as it is a form of positive reinforcement. You lay out the facts and benefits of participating in these exercises.

- **Bribe them:** You might not have to do this forever but for the beginning, you can convince participation with the promise of a reward at the end.

- **Mirror them:** When you mirror their fear and reluctance, you are establishing a connection again. Speak with them and let them know that this hurt will remain unless you try everything you can.

- **Employ heart chakra:** There is a technique recommended by Carol Tuttle that involves "connecting with the heart chakra" (2020). So, basically, you hold your hand on your chest and recite something that reassures your inner child. For example, "You are safe, and letting go of this habit is part of our healing."

Importance of Challenging Resistance

Consider this part of the battle as one between yourself and your inner child. When you allow them to convince you not to participate in these healing activities, you give them the power to keep both of you in a pattern of self-destruction. The reason I use such harsh phrasing is because many of the habits created by your inner child are destructive to your growth and liberation.

Remember that your inner child is a version of yourself that was created out of trauma during childhood. Would you blindly follow a traumatized child on the road to recovery? Of course not! Most of the exercises you're expected to do will, without a doubt, cause your inner child immense distress, but at the end of the day, you know they're necessary. This is where you take advantage of the fact that you're the adult in this, and you need to be in the driver's seat. Still, be kind, understanding, and patient with your inner child, as their intention is and always will be to protect you.

Breaking Self-Sabotaging Habits

Recognizing self-sabotaging behaviors and thought patterns is crucial to embracing and healing your wounded inner child. These behaviors manifest as procrastination, self-doubt, perfectionism, or avoidance of meaningful relationships. Negative self-talk, feelings of unworthiness, and fear of failure or rejection are common thought patterns to look out for. Notice instances where you may be hindering your own success or joy, as these signal tendencies towards self-sabotage.

It is essential to uncover the underlying reasons behind your self-sabotaging actions, as these behaviors often originate from childhood traumas and emotional scars that have been left unaddressed. Take time to contemplate your past experiences and the influences of parents, caregivers, or any other important individuals. Were you subjected to severe criticism or faced neglect and emotional absence? These encounters may instill feelings of inadequacy and a reluctance to be vulnerable, prompting self-sabotage as a misguided form of protection against harm, humiliation, or failure.

The only way out of this toxic habit is to establish new, healthy habits to replace self-sabotaging ones. You can achieve this by setting small, achievable goals and celebrating your progress, as this reinforces positive change and builds confidence. Practice self-compassion and patience, understanding that change is a gradual process and setbacks are part of the journey.

Embracing Change With Open Arms

Change emerges as both a daunting challenge and a powerful ally in almost every aspect of life. Even positive transformations can evoke feelings of fear and uncertainty. This is simply because it's ingrained in our DNA to fear the unknown, and with change comes the unknown.

Embracing change should be viewed as a steadfast companion throughout your healing process. You need to learn how to let go of that extreme need for control. First and foremost, you should recognize that change, although intimidating, is an integral part of growth and healing. For this reason, adopting a mindset that views change as a **catalyst** for positive transformation rather than a source of apprehension will be yet another mighty weapon to add to your arsenal. Embracing change involves cultivating an attitude of openness and receptivity to new experiences and perspectives.

To navigate the **precarious** terrain of change effectively, we can employ various techniques aimed at adaptation and resilience. One such strategy is to establish small, achievable goals. Breaking down the process of change into manageable steps not only makes it less overwhelming but also instills a sense of accomplishment with each milestone achieved. Furthermore, seeking support from trusted friends, family members, or professionals can provide invaluable guidance and encouragement. These people are helpful in many ways and can offer insight, validation, and a sense of belonging.

Another indispensable tool for adapting to change is regular reflection on your progress. You should make time for introspection and allow yourself opportunities to celebrate successes, identify areas for growth, and reassess your approach as needed. By acknowledging and affirming progress, you maintain momentum and stay anchored amidst the ups and downs of change.

You know, very often, people don't even realize that they have a deep-seated fear of change and have convinced themselves that the reluctance they feel is simply a sign of them sticking to their principles or things they like. This is so incorrect, that I'd even go as far as saying it's denial. Acknowledging your own aversion to change is imperative to find ways to embrace it. Have a look at the signs discussed in detail below that you are afraid of change and if you relate to any of them, chances are you have an issue with welcoming change.

Do I Fear Change?

Before we dive into this section, know that a fear of change doesn't necessarily mean you have a phobia. You might think you've found a loophole, thinking, "Well, if I'm not crippled by the idea of change, then this doesn't apply to me." Well, yes, it might. Even if what you experience doesn't bring all your activities to a halt, you might still have a subconscious fear of change. And that too needs work.

Here are some of the reactions you can use as a checklist or guideline:

Forecasting

Forecasting refers to the act of coming up with your own version of events that you believe are sure to occur should you do something. Of course, there is positive forecasting, but in this case, I'm talking about negative forecasting. This is when you jump to conclusions about everything that will go wrong. I say "will" because you're convinced that the outcomes you've predicted are sure to happen, even when you have no proof or reasons to believe that.

Physical Effects

As you can tell, this here refers to physical changes and reactions to the idea of change. While you can experience any unusual or unexpected physical reactions, you're typically riddled with chronic headaches, stomach aches, running tummy, and disruptions to your sleeping patterns.

Panic Attacks

Panic attacks can be quite scary and often lead the person experiencing them to feel a number of physical and psychological symptoms. These symptoms include shortness of breath, chest pain caused by an increased heart rate, sweating, and overwhelming nervousness. Here, you might also begin obsessing over "what ifs," meaning you're running a series of possible outcomes in your head and most of them end badly.

Go Above and Beyond to Gain Control

Even though you're aware of the fact that change cannot be controlled, once you learn each new detail about the specific change, you try to regain control. You do this by desperately trying to control smaller aspects of the larger picture and in doing so, force yourself to try to be perfect. This will eventually lead to burnout and, oftentimes, leave you feeling even more out of control than before.

These effects could lead to:

- fear of life in the future

- isolation

- heart palpitations

- fear of career change even when you're unhappy in your current one

- fear of changing routines

- fear of new relationships, even when your current one is unfulfilling

- substance use and abuse

- depression

- suicide or self-harm

If any of this resonates with you, it might be time to admit that you have a problem with or reluctance to change. Whenever the unknown has got you down, re-read this chapter and remind yourself of what these changes mean to you and will mean to your inner child as a motivating factor to push through even when presented with all these symptoms.

Above all, I emphasize the importance of patience and self-compassion throughout this journey. Once again, healing is not a **linear** process; setbacks and challenges are inevitable. Remind yourself that each step forward, no matter how small, is a testament to your strength and resilience. By embracing change with open arms, you can harness its transformative power. Through small, achievable goals, support from your trusted circle, and regular reflection, it becomes much easier to navigate change, emerge stronger, and bring you closer to rebirth.

Chapter 6:

Mending Relationships

As you navigate the uncharted territory of change, healing, and growth, you will also notice a significant shift in past, present, and future relationships. That being said, these shifts don't just occur; they need to be cultivated, nurtured, acknowledged, and appreciated. This chapter is aimed at helping you discover how healing your inner child can transform your relationships, leading to deeper connections, forgiveness, and the ability to develop healthier bonds.

Reflecting on Relationship Patterns

Take a good look at the quality of the relationships you currently have and may have had in the past. What do you see? Is there any connection between all those relationships? Are there any similarities between the individuals or the relationship dynamics? You may not be able to answer these questions at the top of your head, but I can say with almost 100% certainty that they all share a common factor!

Whether it is codependency, distance, control, or various other elements that comprise unhealthy or even toxic relationships, wounded inner children often have the most influence here. This section will delve a bit deeper into the nature of your relationship skills and unearth some issues you may not have known existed. Before we do anything, please understand that no matter what we discover about your relationship trends and habits, it's not your fault. The dysfunction or **in cohesion** we're exposed to leaves permanent scars that trail us all the way into adulthood. Many of us accept that this is the way we are and believe there's no way to change it, so we continue on a never-ending cycle of failed or unfulfilling relationships. My goal is to help you determine any problem areas and provide practical strategies to help you break free from them.

The Where and Why

Knowing where it all started is a major breakthrough to help zero in on why those encounters imprinted themselves in your character. Since these habits are usually developed in childhood, your family's communication skills and examples of how to handle certain emotions would have given rise to your complex perceptions.

Here are some things to keep in mind when reflecting on how these traits may have been born:

Did your family communicate effectively?

Were they able to address all emotions as valid and relevant?

Who was the primary leader in family communication?

Do you think these communication methods have shaped any of your own communication preferences and abilities?

Are there any things you do that resemble the communication styles from your childhood?

Do any of these resemblances surface in any of your current relationships? If yes, how do they impact those relationships?

Have outside communication trends triggered any intense emotions in you? If yes, how did you address those triggers?

Name specific outcomes of your own communication skills. Ascertain if they are positive or negative.

Do you communicate well during disagreements or moments of conflict? Do you think this relates directly to the communication styles you were exposed to during childhood?

What have you learned when comparing your own communication style with that of your parents?

Is there anything you think requires change?

Knowing if anything requires change is so important because many of us think there's nothing wrong with the way we do things only because this is all we've ever known. This is not to say that elements from our past are all bad, but the way our inner child receives and perceives those moments tremendously shapes our actions and feelings towards certain things as adults.

Since we can't go through life-avoiding relationships, it's important to note that your upbringing influences the quality of your friendships and acquaintanceships, as well as your romantic, familial, and professional relationships.

One simply has to take a closer look at the current relationships you have to establish what they say about your upbringing. Some people are drawn to chaos and attract toxicity in friends, family, romantic partners, and even coworkers. Others, on the other hand, tend to surround themselves with powerful people. Perhaps they've developed an incessant need to feel protected by someone and to cling to any form of authority. These are all signs of a relationship pattern mirroring our past.

Relationship OCD

Relationship OCD, or R-OCD, is a relatively new concept, and not many people know they're suffering from it. Have you ever found yourself in a relationship where the person is so good for you but you're completely incapable of connecting with them on a deeper level? You know you care about them and don't want to be with them, but you simply can't feel that overwhelming love and need to have them around. You may be suffering from relationship OCD. This can be a nasty little demon that's also a result of childhood wounds.

What is R-OCD?

In simple terms, R-OCD is just like a normal obsessive-compulsive disorder; however, it relates directly to your romantic or social relationships. You have perpetual **intrusive** thoughts, and no matter what you do, you can't get rid of them. They often result in continuously failing relationships or you being the toxic one in your relationship.

A lot of people suffering from R-OCD already know someone isn't right with them, but they are so confused that they feel they can't talk to anyone about this. This is a serious, but underestimated condition.

Let's look at some of the signs of R-OCD:

- constant thoughts that you're settling for your partner; always feeling like you could get better

- constant questioning or doubting about your partner's true feelings for you; don't believing they really love you

- gnawing feelings that you are not truly connecting with your partner as other couples are

- persistently needing to be reassured of your partner's love and devotion

- obsessing over your partner's imperfections

- looking for any reason to end your relationship with your partner

- feeling unworthy of love

While it's impossible to pinpoint the exact causes of R-OCD, there are many factors that influence its emergence and progression, like *serotonin* imbalance in the brain, changes in general brain chemistry, or significant, unexpected life events like tragedy. Other factors, like losing someone close to you, experiencing abuse in childhood, or general trauma, can also result in the development of R-OCD.

I want you to focus on the last point here, general trauma, as this is the bracket where wounded inner children fall. Since trauma relates to anything that causes significant emotional, physical, and psychological damage, we cannot say for sure what counts as trauma and what doesn't. Yes, physical abuse is traumatic and causes extreme psychological responses, but simply being yelled at has the potential to evoke the same emotions, depending on the individual.

If you've been victimized in any way, you may grow up to develop R-OCD, and this could result in poor relationship skills. Once you've established that you're suffering from this, or even suspect it, you need to take affirmative action to heal.

Managing R-OCD

With the help of therapy, medication, and various other interventions, you can live a happier and more fulfilling life. Below are some ways that you can ease your symptoms.

Communicate

Communication really does do wonders, as you are open and honest about your fears as well as the extent of your abilities. Speak to those close to you and let them know what you're going through and what they can do to make things easier for you. These don't have to be excessive or outrageous requests; simple things like accepting when your social battery is empty and allowing you to retreat to your safe space without making you feel guilty are some of the easiest things they can do.

Include Your Partner

Take the time to prepare for an open discussion with your partner about the challenges you face in your relationship. Let them know that none of this is their fault and that you are trying to manage your disorder. Advise them on how they can help. An important part of this step is to listen to your partner too. Yes, you are trying to recover from the damage caused by matters that were out of your control, but the burden of undoing that damage cannot be placed solely on your partner. They deserve to have their feelings acknowledged and you should handle them with patience because, more often than not, our partners can't fully grasp the severity of this disorder and sometimes minimize the effects it has on us. This could lead to arguments but as much as you'd like them to see things from your perspective, try and view things from theirs.

Involve a Professional

Yep, I'm mentioning professional assistance again. As capable and tough as we'd like to believe we are, no one can do everything by themselves. R-OCD is such a profound condition and while there are ways to manage it, it's rare that you can completely abolish it. The challenges usually present themselves after you're already trying to make the changes needed to cope and you tend to feel like a failure when you relapse. This is where you can get a professional involved. There are various forms of therapeutic techniques to help, but sometimes simply connecting with others who are facing the same issues as you makes all the difference. You can attend group sessions, whether online or in person, or simply join online support chat services where you interact with others just like you without subjecting yourself to the vulnerability you fear.

Intolerance of Others

This is another effect of childhood trauma in adult relationships. Growing up in an environment where we witness the blatant irritability or intolerance of significant others and their unique habits cultivates the same intolerance of our own significant others. We tend to get annoyed easily by certain quirks they may have and instead of addressing it healthily and from a place of patience and understanding, we lash out or become irrationally critical of them and make them feel insufferable. This is because we've rationalized those behaviors and often don't understand why our significant others are so upset or hurt by our actions, leading to a perception of them that is weak or overly sensitive.

Inability to Resolve Conflict

This is because we haven't learned any conflict resolution skills from our parents or caregivers. You might be someone who has had many failed relationships that typically could have been saved, but inability to navigate healthy ways to **reconcile** after differences in opinion or disagreements led to failure. These individuals often watch helplessly as meaningful relationships fall apart and have no idea how to go about fixing them.

Settling

Habits like settling are not only bad for yourself but also for the other person. You know that your relationship is going nowhere, or you can clearly see that your relationship has no positive results, yet you choose to remain with that person because you've developed the habit of accepting that anything is better than nothing. Perhaps you even believe that you can't get better or don't deserve better, so instead of looking for something better, you make do with what you have. This simply leads to emptiness and loneliness.

Commitment Issues

You're desperately in need of the assurance that you can leave whenever you want. This could be a result of abandonment by a parent or caregiver. You feel committing leaves you vulnerable to being abandoned again, and, of course, you'd rather not commit because that way it doesn't hurt that bad when things end.

Control Issues

Here, you're likely an individual who would rather take full control of a relationship than leave yourself at the will of another. You may have trusted someone who disappointed you and you're determined to be in control of their actions, etc. Perhaps you're not dictating their lives, but you take control over certain large relationship matters, like finances. This means you probably pay for everything because you don't want to rely on another person.

Cheating

This is often the result of not feeling loved and valued as a child. It typically results in an inability to feel truly fulfilled and accepted in a relationship. This incessant need to be assured as someone who is worthy of love can result in having multiple partners simultaneously. You might also engage in this behavior out of fear of being hurt.

Incessant Need for Alone Time

This might seem normal, and to a certain extent, it is. It's only when this need for time by yourself exceeds time with others, especially if you're in a relationship, that it becomes a problem and a symptom. You come across as simply pushing them away or appearing to not want to spend time with them. This is generally the outcome of growing up in an environment of chaos. You're probably in a constant state of anxiety and stress that you rely on excessive time alone to calm those fears.

To end this section, encourage yourself to actively choose relationships that align with your values and support your healing journey. Make sure that you are setting and maintaining your boundaries, as this helps in recognizing and responding to red flags in interactions with others. By empowering yourself to reflect on your relationship patterns and take proactive steps towards change, you equip yourself with the tools needed to foster healthier connections and cultivate fulfilling relationships on your path to healing and personal growth.

The Power of Forgiveness

This topic can be quite controversial, especially when it comes to forgiving people who have hurt you. I want to be very clear from the get-go about what forgiveness means. You are not forgiving the person's actions; you are simply allowing yourself to let go of the anger and hurt caused by those actions.

Forgiveness is not only to set yourself free of the burden of carrying that heaviness on your heart; it's also intended to educate the wrongdoer. They need to see that their actions will not define or consume you. Forgiving the people who hurt you sends the message that you have risen above their influence. They did something bad and expected you to do something bad in return (whether it's hate them, bad mouth them, or physically hurt them). Choosing to forgive takes an enormous amount of strength and courage. This is because your natural instinct is to respond to the negative emotions that fill you when you think about it or even hear their name. Imagine how strong you are when every fiber of your being compels you to act out of hurt and rage, yet you act out of forgiveness and release. This strength is undeniable.

Forgiveness allows you to reclaim your power and move forward with greater clarity and peace. Choosing to embrace forgiveness is a transformative tool on your healing journey, as it empowers you to cultivate deeper compassion for yourself and others. It is the epitome of self-love.

Healthy Relationships Moving Forward

When you work on healing your inner child, you create the opportunity for better and more satisfying relationships. Healing your inner child gives you the strength to approach relationships with a new sense of understanding, kindness, and authenticity.

Let's explore the characteristics of healthy relationships:

Communication

This doesn't only mean talking. Communication entails communicating openly and honestly and being willing to be vulnerable for the betterment of your relationship.

Consensualism

This is not limited to **consensual** intimacy; it applies to all aspects of your relationship. The social engagements you're expected to be involved in, as well as any other activity pertaining to your relationship, should be mutually welcomed and enjoyed.

Boundaries

Boundaries are so important because we all like and dislike different things. You can't be too scared that your partner will leave or be mad at you for not liking something and allow it to completely disregard your boundaries.

Trust

This isn't something that comes easy, and having someone's full trust is often underappreciated. Think about how difficult it is to earn your trust, so it goes without saying that you would also have to put in the work to earn your partner's trust. The people you have relationships with should be the ones you are most comfortable being vulnerable around, and this can only be achieved through trust.

Good relationships are built on respect, communication, and shared values. In healthy relationships, people respect each other's boundaries, thoughts, and feelings. There is a feeling of fairness and mutual respect where both individuals feel appreciated and listened to. Effective communication is crucial for healthy relationships as it allows you to express your needs, wishes, and concerns as individuals in a safe and supportive environment. Shared values create a sense of unity and harmony, creating deeper bonds and mutual understanding.

Take time to think about the qualities that matter to you in a relationship and what you are willing to **reciprocate**. Defining your goals will help you attract and nurture relationships that match your values and goals.

Have a look at the below elements essential for developing healthy relationships:

- **Self-awareness:** Helps you identify patterns and behaviors that could damage your relationships.

- **Self-care:** Ensures that you prioritize your well-being and promote self-confidence and a positive self-image.

- **Boundaries:** Helps you establish healthy limits and protect your physical and emotional welfare.

That said, your responsibility is also to listen attentively to your partner's feelings, thoughts, and experiences without judgment or interruption. Be sure to empathize with their emotions and opinions, as this demonstrates a desire to understand rather than only be understood. This level of empathy cultivates a strong connection and mutual support.

It's crucial to continue honoring your inner child as you navigate healthy relationships. Choose relationships that bring you joy, growth, and fulfillment while avoiding those that perpetuate old wounds or negative habits. Always trust your instincts and be mindful of how you feel around others; in other words, keep listening to the voice of your inner child. Don't allow yourself to long so much for a deep connection that you dismiss signs of toxicity or potential red flags. Surround yourself with people who uplift and motivate you and are willing to put the same amount of effort as you into cultivating mutually satisfying connections.

Chapter 7:

Maintaining Your Inner Child Healing

This chapter not only highlights what you've already learned about your journey to inner child restoration, but it also contains a range of practical strategies and insights aimed at integrating the healing process into your daily life. Herein, you'll find advice that promotes resilience and growth and will help you achieve and sustain joy amidst life's inevitable trials. Through a deliberate and mindful approach, you will learn to cultivate a nurturing environment that not only supports your inner child's recovery but also empowers you to confront and overcome recurring challenges.

Integrating Healing Into Everyday Life

Many of us tend to fall back into old habits or simply do away with new, learned habits that are beneficial to our well-being. The reasons behind this obviously differ from person to person; however, one thing is certain: we're undoing all our hard work. As I've repeatedly mentioned throughout this book, healing cannot be achieved through a few exercises, and then, because you notice a shift in your mood and positive changes to your attitude and outlook on life, you assume all the work's been done and you can now stop all activities related to this journey—since you've reached your destination.

Unfortunately, this couldn't be further from the truth. Your journey is one that never ends. In fact, you might find yourself a few steps back after some time, in which case you'd have to relearn some of the introductory steps of your healing process. I know some of you might be thinking, "Well, this is not going to be me," or "Whoever finds themselves going backward instead of forward is not strong enough for healing," but I need to tell you that you'd be surprised how many people find themselves in this position a year or two into their healing.

This setback, in itself, is one that should be embraced and welcomed as an opportunity to learn and perhaps change course or perspective. Setbacks are not the end nor should they be seen as evidence that we're incapable of regaining control over our lives. If anything, they are a testament to our humanity and should be used as stepping stones to a journey greater than the one we set out for to begin with. We can transform setbacks and challenges into catalysts for greater goals. For instance, let's say your goal at the end of this journey was to reconnect with your parents, but they were unwilling to do their part. Now, you could give up and leave the blame on them for not being interested in rectifying their past mistakes, or you could use their reluctance to get in touch with **estranged** family members and old family friends. After putting in all the work, who knows, you might find that you not only reconnected yourself with your parents and various other members of your family, but you also opened the door for everyone else to reunite and hash out issues from the past.

The key is to not give up and ensure you prioritize all activities and exercises relating to your healing journey.

The Continuous Process

I don't want to sound like a broken record but I must stress the importance of setting aside time daily to work on your inner child's healing. This not only means you'll definitely have allocated, uninterrupted time to focus on your self-care, but it also automatically reinforces the message to your inner child that their well-being is at the top of your to-do list.

But how will you find the time in your busy schedule? Well, there are some activities that can be done in the mornings before you start your day, others can be done during your lunch break at work, and some can even be done before bed. Only you know what demands your days consist of, so you should actually take a moment to do a daily planner and allocate at least 15 minutes in the morning and 15 minutes in the evening to your inner child's work.

Now that we've covered that, let's jump straight into some activities to integrate into your life.

Journal Fever

Journaling has come up quite a lot in terms of healing lately, and I understand why. It really works! Do you have any idea how powerful it is to write something down and bring it into **fruition**? It's like how some people are overcome with feelings of **euphoria** when they create a to-do list or even a grocery checklist, and as you attend to each task or get each item on the list, you check it off to confirm it's done. It feels incredible.

Similarly, journaling, or any form of expressive writing, has been found to reduce anxiety, depression, and general stress. That's right, science has actually revealed that this activity engages both hemispheres in the brain as it stimulates communication between all areas responsible for mood regulation. This must be why we feel so clear-headed and in touch with our emotions after doing so (*The Science of Journaling: How Writing Benefits Your Brain*, n.d.). It doesn't matter if you've never written anything before in your life; practice makes perfect and you'll enjoy the psychological benefits regardless.

Here are some of the benefits linked to writing and journaling (*The Science of Journaling: How Writing Benefits Your Brain*, n.d.):

- boosts creativity

- fosters personal growth

- encourages self-reflection

- improves mental aptitude

- assists with recalling old memories

- bolsters problem-solving abilities

Different Types of Journals

You can have multiple journals; in fact, I recommend that you have different journals for different things. Below are some focused journal ideas:

Self-Love

Will be used to remind ourselves that we deserve compassion, kindness, and love. You can add prompts like:

> *Today I will forgive myself for* [fill in the blank]

> *The three things I admire about myself today are* [fill in the blank]

Gratitude

Will be to remind yourself of the things you are blessed with. This promotes thankfulness and gratitude. You can add prompts like:

> *Today I am grateful for these three things* [fill in the blank]

> *I am grateful for this event from my past* [fill in the blank] as it has taught me [fill in the blank]

This difficult experience [fill in the blank] *propelled me to achieve* [fill in the blank]

Self-Esteem

Used to highlight qualities you like about yourself as well as those that others like about you. You can choose prompts like:

> *Today I was complimented on my* [fill in the blank]

> *I appreciate my ability to* [fill in the blank]

> *These are the qualities my family admires about me* [fill in the blank]

Of course, there'll be days when you're a little stumped and really need to dig deep, but with practice, you'll learn that there's so much to appreciate and love around you and about yourself that it'll come to you naturally.

Mindful Meditation

Mindfulness involves being fully aware of your innermost feelings, your surroundings, your thoughts, and so forth. Allowing yourself to reach complete relaxation makes it possible for you to tend to your inner child and listen for anything that could be disrupting your inner peace.

How you'll do it:

- Find a quiet, tranquil space.

- Control your breathing until it's slow, deep, and intentional.

- Close your eyes as you envision the child within you.

- Begin a dialogue with them as you would with a friend or family member.

- Ask them questions like:

- "How are you today?"

- "Is there anything you want to share with me?"

- "Is there anything that made you particularly happy today?"

- Don't limit your conversation to fears and worries. Allow your inner child to share positives about their healing as well, and be open about your own conscious feelings towards life in general.

You can combine your meditation with *Metta meditation*. These are basically just loving phrases directed at yourself during mediation to foster self-compassion and kindness.

Here are some Metta meditation phrases you can use (Ellen | EKT Creatives-Spiritual Business Girlie, 2022):

May I be free from fear, anxiety, anger, and all afflictions.

May I learn to identify the sources of anger, longing, paranoia, and delusion in myself.

May I be safe and free from injury.

May I develop a healthy disconnect from attachment and aversion.

May I learn how to nourish the seeds of joy in myself every day.

May I be peaceful, happy, and light in body and spirit.

Positive Affirmations

Affirmations are yet another newly found tool that's been said to work wonders on the psyche and emotional **reparation**. This is something you should be able to do every morning and every evening before bed. While you can say these out loud anywhere, it really solidifies the words uttered when you look at yourself in the mirror and speak so compassionately to yourself.

It's important to tailor your affirmations to your own needs, but any positive affirmations that build self-acceptance, self-esteem, and self-love will do.

Here are some affirmations you can start using right now:

I am beautiful on the inside and out.

I love who I am without the need for the approval of others.

I do my best and give my all every single day.

There is always room for improvement, but that does not mean that I am not enough.

Learning is a privilege, not a burden.

I do not run from my past; I embrace it and learn from it.

My experiences, both good and bad, have shaped the amazing person I am today.

Every day is a new day to be stronger and wiser than I was yesterday.

My love for myself is not defined by material possessions or accomplishments in life.

I am human, and mistakes are a natural part of learning.

I can achieve anything I put my mind to.

I am not a victim of trauma but a conqueror of my hardships.

I do not have to apologize for putting my own well-being first.

Child-Like Fun

Do you remember any of the games you enjoyed playing as a child? Perhaps you liked doing puzzles or family game nights. Reintroducing these fun and games from your past is another way to not only connect with your inner child but it can produce the same results as reparenting.

By creating new, positive memories in the same setting, you reframe your subconscious reactions towards those experiences.

Continued Growth and Self-Discovery

Embrace this lifelong journey, as the benefits and rewards from this commitment will flow over from yourself to your children and their children, and so the cycle continues. We hear about generational curses and damage that gets passed on from generation to generation all the time, but why can't we create a positive version of that form of inheritance? Let our personal growth and continued learning and development inspire all those we connect with so that we can leave a legacy of power for ourselves.

Continued growth can only be achieved through consistency and a willingness to explore all avenues that may produce exceptional results. It's about being afraid but doing it anyway. That's what it means to be brave. Bravery doesn't mean you're **devoid** of fear or immune to it. No, bravery means facing something head-on despite feelings of fear and anxiety.

How to Remain on the Path of Continued Growth

Consider your healing journey as you embark on a continual voyage of self-awareness and growth. Just as seasons change, so too does your inner landscape, which is constantly shifting and evolving. Embracing this endless journey with an open heart and mind is fundamental to sustaining the progress you've made.

Here are some recommended tips to help you along:

Embrace Opportunities for Growth

Don't shy away from experiences that act as chances for personal growth and self-exploration. Encourage yourself to participate in endeavors that push your boundaries, spark your curiosity, and fuel your enthusiasm. Explore new interests that stretch your limits, such as acquiring a musical skill, experimenting with art, or immersing yourself in photography. These activities nurture creativity and provide avenues for self-expression and discovery. You might be surprised to find that these new opportunities can steer your whole life in a completely different direction.

Pursue Educational Opportunities

We all know that education is a powerful tool for personal development and self-discovery. Welcome opportunities that promise to expand your knowledge and skills in areas that interest you. Whether it's enrolling in a course, attending workshops, or pursuing further academic studies, the pursuit of knowledge enriches your understanding of yourself and the world around you. By feeding your curiosity and thirst for learning, you empower yourself to navigate life with greater confidence and enlightenment. This, of course, also means that you are equipped to advise others and guide them on a path towards their own healing and development.

Remain Open to New Experiences

This one can be quite tricky, especially if you have an inherent apprehension toward change. That said, you will be responsible for finding ways to help you push through because life is full of opportunities for growth and transformation, but they generally lie beyond the boundaries of familiarity. Your comfort zone is typically one of isolation, repetition, and limits, so the only way to broaden your horizons is to remain open to new experiences that challenge your perceptions. Wherever possible, travel to unfamiliar places, immerse yourself in diverse communities and cultures or participate in activities that you've never considered before. These experiences not only diversify your life but also deepen your understanding of who you are and what your inner child needs.

Mindfulness in Action

Mindfulness is crucial on this journey. You need to learn to stay attuned to your inner child's reactions and feelings as you **traverse** new experiences. A magnificent way to do this is by cultivating self-awareness through regular check-ins with yourself, acknowledging your emotions, and honoring your needs. Practicing mindfulness in action allows you to create a nurturing environment where your inner child can not only heal but also thrive.

Navigating Setbacks With Grace

We all know that setbacks are a natural part of life. They cannot be anticipated, so they cannot be avoided. So this is where I hit you with the harsh reality that, despite your best efforts, there may come times when old wounds resurface, triggering emotions and memories from the past that we likely don't want to relive. Dealing with these setbacks gracefully and with resilience is essential.

Let's have a walkthrough of some of the ways that you can help navigate these setbacks with grace.

Reframe Your Mind

Yes, it feels terrible when we encounter a setback and we often find ourselves frozen in a state of self-loathing and hopelessness. But I want you to view this stagnation and self-pity or self-hatred as an injustice to your inner child. They're counting on you to get back on your feet, dust yourself off, and keep moving forward.

I've said it before, and I'll say it a million times more: setbacks are not signs of failure but rather invitations for a new perspective that can lead to unprecedented opportunities and experiences. Now I know that when you're faced with obstacles, it's natural to feel flustered, overwhelmed, discouraged, or even ashamed. You might be riddled with questions about what you did wrong. However, reframing your idea of setbacks as opportunities allows you to approach them with openness and curiosity.

Instead of devoting your time to avoiding discomfort, lean into it, embracing the chance to explore unresolved emotions and patterns from your past that you may have long forgotten or didn't even know existed. This reframed mindset allows you to reclaim agency over your healing journey and cultivate resilience in the face of adversity.

Learn to Self-Soothe

When confronted with triggers, self-soothing techniques offer a sense of comfort and stability. Deep breathing exercises may be simple and easy to do, yet they are a powerful way to bring your nervous system back to calmness and help ground yourself in the present moment.

They involve taking intentionally slow, deep breaths while focusing on the sensation of air entering and exiting your body. Alternatively, you can participate in activities that bring joy and relaxation, whether it's spending time in nature, practicing mindfulness meditation, or listening to relaxing music.

Try this deep breathing exercise to get you started:

Alternate Nostril Breathing

You can perform this technique whenever you feel stressed but be sure to be in a quiet space. It's said to produce the best results when done on an empty stomach but can be done at any time.

1. Get into a comfortable sitting position.

2. Close your right nostril with your thumb after a deep exhale. Keep it there.

3. Inhale through your left nostril.

4. Now use your index finger to close your left nostril and inhale deeply.

5. And release.

6. Continue this alternating breathing technique for 5–10 minutes.

7. Make sure you end with an exhale from the left nostril.

Seek Support From Your Community

The intention behind seeking support from your community is not to expose your darkest secrets or force you to be vulnerable to the public; it's to demonstrate that you don't have to navigate the challenges of healing alone.

Your community—whether friends, family, or support groups—can offer invaluable support and encouragement along your journey. All you have to do is ask. Reach out to those you trust and who you know can hold space for your emotions without judgment and provide comfort and validation when you need it most. Additionally, you should consider seeking guidance from a mental health professional who specializes in inner-child healing, as this can actually be regarded as a field or branch of its own.

Professional support offers a safe and confidential space to explore your experiences, gain insight into underlying trends, and develop coping strategies for managing setbacks effectively. Remember, seeking help is a sign of strength, not weakness, and obtaining support is an essential aspect of your healing journey. You are proving to yourself and your inner child that you are devoted to their well-being and recovery.

Chapter 8:

Living With Joy and Wholeness

As daunting and unattainable as the idea of being free from the wounds of our past may appear, I'm here to tell you that you can do it. There's absolutely nothing beyond your reach in terms of this journey toward healing, happiness, and wholeness. Once you decide to take your first step on this profound path towards living a life **suffused** with joy and wholeness, you open yourself to the wonders of endless possibility.

This chapter delves into the transformative process of nurturing and integrating your inner child, recognizing them as the cornerstones of a fulfilled and harmonious existence. By mending the wounds of your past with compassionate understanding, you gradually work your way to self-fulfillment and an unparalleled sense of completeness. Embracing this venture not only fosters a deeper relationship with oneself but also produces richer connections with others, grounded in authenticity and empathy. As you navigate the terrain of healing, you begin to observe the blossoming of pure joy and contentment within. The beauty of this is that, in time, this joy and bliss start radiating outward and eventually flow over into every facet of your life. The benefits of achieving such wholeness are innumerable, as they offer a sanctuary of **repose** amidst life's **tumult** and a reservoir of resilience in facing its challenges.

Reclaiming Joy in Your Life

Joy is such an underrated gift. We've become so set in our ways of building an impressive professional portfolio, seeing to responsibilities, then going to sleep, and doing it all over again the next day that we've lost sight of the fact that joy is not only possible but essential to our lives. Do you remember being a child and only worrying about having fun and enjoying the time you had? Seriously, what's it going to take for us to realize that being responsible doesn't mean we have to sacrifice the very things that make life worth living?

No matter how busy your life is, all of us should carve out some time for fun and judgment-free pleasure. Let's discuss some activities that are sure to reignite the childish flame inside you.

Playground Fun

That's right. I'm taking you way back to your roots. Whether you have a pet you're taking for some playtime, a child who needs to burn their energy, or you're just taking a stroll in the park, I'm sure every now and then you find yourself at a playground. And what better time to unleash your inner child than then?

Play on the slides, swings, merry-go-round, and anything else your playground has to offer. Playing is so important for adults as it not only reduces stress and keeps you young at heart, it forces you to be physically active, which comes with an array of health benefits of its own, and it strengthens social connections. It also stimulates creativity and bolsters the general function of your brain.

Cycling

Riding a bike with the intention to remain fit and healthy is a good motivator but for those who aren't looking to make cycling their daily exercise outlet, just ride to have fun! Cycling has an abundance of health benefits; being so much fun is just a bonus. When you ride a bike regularly, you're not only having a good time; you're also working on your muscle strength, as all your muscle groups are engaged when cycling. This is probably why it's such a great way to improve stamina. Another great thing about choosing cycling as a recreational activity is that it can take you to marvelous new locations that you may not even have known existed in your surrounding areas. Other benefits include better posture, an improved mood, better joint health, helping you lose weight, and generally just a great **cardiovascular** workout. So, why not do something that's fun and good for you?

Splish Splashing

I can't tell you how many times I've seen parents at the water park or swimming pools with their kids and only a handful are actually in the water, having a blast. Why do we do this to ourselves? Yeah, kids love swimming, and we mainly bring them to these places so they can have a good time, but why are we denying ourselves that? I say we embrace the gift of being alive and capable of doing things that we enjoy and dive into the bliss of aquatic thrills. Swimming is not only a full-body workout that burns tons of calories, improves lung function, promotes heart health, and stimulates muscle growth; it also improves mental health and strengthens cognitive function. But most importantly, it leads to healthy aging! So, next time you're at the swimming pools, don't let society's perception of what activities should be for adults and what should be for children hold you back; you go down that monster slide or you swim like you're about to win an Olympic medal, because there's no age restriction on fun.

Back to Nature

Now, I know camping isn't for everyone, but I promise you, you will return home with a new appreciation for life. Spending time in nature has been scientifically proven to enhance cognitive function, mental prowess, and general physical fitness. The smell of the air also releases feel-good chemicals in your brain, which is why you'll experience reduced stress and anxiety when outdoors. You will also find new tips and tricks to manage time outdoors and pass those skills on to those around you. The sound of nature at work is also a great way to ensure you get quality sleep without the need for a white noise machine. So, don't wait. Start preparing for your camping trip now and watch how your family returns closer, healthier, and happier.

For those who really aren't keen on camping, hiking can achieve similar results. Hiking in nature can just as easily get your muscle groups engaged, get those lungs working, and, at the same time, allow time for reflection and spiritual enlightenment.

Paintballing

For those who don't know, imagine paintballing as a fun team sport where you shoot paintballs at your friends to get them out. It's played outdoors and indoors, often with cool game missions like capturing the flag. You gear up, dodge obstacles, and have a blast. It's not just fun; it's a great workout that boosts fitness and agility. Plus, it helps you think strategically, work in a team, and de-stress. It's like giving your inner child a fun and wild adventure while bonding with friends and family, as well as letting off steam!

Learning to Play an Instrument

Playing an instrument is about picking up skills to make music on stuff like piano, guitar, violin, or drums. You take lessons, practice loads, and get good at techniques and tunes. It's not just about the music; it helps boost motor skills, brainpower, and emotional well-being. Playing an instrument can bring back childhood dreams, allow you to express yourself, and give you a fun and fulfilling hobby. It's like giving your inner child a chance to play, express emotions, and find joy in creating music.

Going to the Arcade

Visiting the arcade is all about having a blast at a place filled with fun games like video games, pinball, and claw machines. It's an exciting spot where you can enjoy a variety of games, improve your reflexes, and solve challenges. Playing at the arcade isn't just fun; it boosts coordination, sharpens your mind, and can make you feel nostalgic and happy. It's like stepping back into your carefree childhood, having a great time, and making fun memories with those close to you.

Hosting Karaoke Nights

Hosting karaoke nights is all about getting together with friends or family to sing your hearts out to your favorite tunes. You can make use of a karaoke machine, but even just doing it on the TV is more than enough to get the fun flowing. It's a fun and supportive way to enjoy music and have a great time. Singing along not only lifts your spirits but also boosts your respiratory health, vocal skills, and confidence. It's a chance to express yourself, destress, and bond with others while belting out your favorite songs. Karaoke nights are like a fun escape to just be yourself, feel connected, and let your inner child shine through without any worries. This could also be the perfect opportunity to combine it with another activity, like learning to play an instrument. Consider this a chance to show off your skills.

Heading to a Trampoline Park

Visiting a trampoline park is like stepping into a fun space filled with bouncy trampolines and foam pits for some jumping fun. It's a total workout that boosts fitness, balance, and strength while also sharpening your focus and spatial skills. Jumping around is not just a good time; it's a stress reliever that brings pure joy. It's like giving your inner child a chance to play freely, let loose, and feel the excitement of bouncing around without a care in the world. Share a carefree laugh and pure bliss with both kids and adults having the time of their lives.

Creating Indoor Obstacle Course Races

Creating indoor obstacle course races is all about setting up fun physical challenges right inside your home. Think of crawling under tables, jumping over cushions, and balancing on beams. It's a great way to boost your fitness, agility, and coordination while also sharpening your problem-solving skills. Plus, it gets your creative juices flowing as you design the course and figure out the best way to tackle it. Emotionally, it's super satisfying and confidence-boosting to complete the course, and it's just plain fun! Doing this can help heal your inner child by bringing back the joy of imaginative play, giving you a sense of adventure, and keeping you active in a playful and exciting way. This is also a great activity to do with your kids and they'll definitely cherish this time together until the end of time.

These activities may sound expensive, but I assure you, somewhere in your budget, there is space for activities that allow you to not only reclaim the joy in your life but also re-parent your wounded inner child. Make new memories that will reframe the perceptions embedded in your inner child. The activity isn't the key; allowing yourself to let go of the expectations of you as an adult, even for a brief moment, is. You deserve to just have mindless fun every once in a while, and your inner child will be eternally grateful.

The Journey to Wholeness

As you have learned, delving into the depths of your inner world involves facing painful truths and rediscovering the innocence of your childhood self. This leads us towards inner peace and self-compassion. The concept of *next* acts as a beacon and highlights the progress made on your healing journey. It symbolizes the transition from woundedness to empowerment, where past traumas no longer have dominion over your present. We embrace self-awareness, self-love, and a sense of wholeness in this new phase.

At the core of inner child healing is adopting practices that promote wholeness. Meditation emerges as a powerful tool and encourages introspection and reconnection. These practices break down barriers created by past traumas as they promote unity and connectivity. Through meditation's tranquility, we nurture unity within ourselves and with the world, cultivating absolute wholeness.

Even with your newfound lease on life, engaging in community activities provides valuable support on the path to healing. Now is the time to surround yourself with supportive companions and ensure your environment fosters a sense of belonging, as this will offer solace through shared experiences and strength through collective resilience. Whether you choose to attain this support network through support groups, creative workshops, or spiritual communities, these communal spaces will not only propel your healing but also reinforce your efforts to achieve inner peace and rebirth.

Self-acceptance and self-love are integral elements needed for this rebirth and embracing compassion liberates you from the chains of guilt, self-blame, self-pity, and shame. Through gentle self-care and positive self-talk, we foster a nurturing relationship with ourselves and allow ourselves to welcome every aspect of who we are with unconditional love and acceptance. As we progress in healing, certain indicators emerge and affirm our growth.

Signs That You Are Healing

Keeping track of your progress is not to be obsessive about recovery; instead, it is to help you look back and see how far you've come and motivate you to keep going. Here are some of the signs you can look for to establish whether your inner child has truly begun their transformation.

Acquired Healthy Coping Strategies

This is something that you won't be checking for soon after embarking on this transformative journey. The majority of your journey is spent first learning to listen to the needs of your inner child and then finding healthy strategies that resonate with you. Once you have this, you'll notice that some of the emotions don't entirely disappear; you have just mastered the art of coping. And this is cause for celebration.

Positive Ways to Regulate Emotions

Here again, the key is to understand that a healed inner child doesn't mean that your intense emotions won't completely disappear. You just find outlets and methods that have provided you with the strength to regulate your emotions in a positive, non-destructive way.

You've Got Boundaries

You're finally at a point where you no longer feel guilty for setting boundaries and the boundaries you've set aim to promote and nurture healing. They prioritize your well-being without being selfish or damaging to those around you.

Self-Care Is No. 1

This means you've established and maintained healthy self-care routines and rituals and adhered to them no matter what. You have a new appreciation for your own well-being and you're able to stick to it.

The Art of Positive Self-Expression is Yours

You have mastered expressing yourself clearly and assertively while remaining respectful. This also means that any unpleasant retaliation or lashing-out habits you may have had are under control.

No More Resistance

So you remember how we talked about your inner child battling with embracing change and vulnerability? Well, this sign is quite obvious because you can literally feel the change within yourself as you no longer feel that unrelenting sensation that compels you to avoid feeling vulnerable and bare.

Compassion Master

You've excelled at showing yourself kindness and compassion. The old habit of jumping straight to extreme self-criticism and berating has been abolished and you now know how to address your own failures and flaws.

Chief of Self-Awareness

After all, this is what all your activities have prepared you for. You are now able to do a full introspection of what you need and which situations and experiences disturb your inner child. This is essential, as you are on a lifelong journey of protecting and caring for them.

Spontaneity and Playfulness Come Naturally

You no longer have to convince yourself to get involved in playful activities or consider them a drag. You welcome them with open arms and look forward to the time you'll spend unwinding and just connecting with your inner child.

Recognizing these signs validates our progress and motivates us to continue nurturing our inner child with tenderness. It's important to remember that these signs may look differently for everyone, and the list I've given you is simply a guideline of the most common and shared byproducts of healed inner children. Don't be alarmed or start searching for flaws in the process if you find that you're not experiencing some of these yet. It might mean that you've still got some work that needs to be done.

Extending Your Healing to Help Others

Extending your healing journey to assist others is a natural progression towards living a life filled with joy and wholeness. As you navigate through your own healing process, you discover the significant impact your personal growth can have on those around you. Many individuals carry silent burdens concealed from the world, grappling with inner demons and unresolved traumas. However, with heightened self-awareness gained through your healing journey, you become sensitive to subtle signs of distress in others—the echoes of wounded inner children seeking solace.

This awareness empowers you to offer compassion and support, shining a beacon of hope for those who are silently struggling. By sharing your healing journey experiences and insights, you have the potential to uplift and inspire others, guiding them towards their own healing and self-discovery paths. Approaching this journey with patience and empathy is essential, as everyone may be battling unseen challenges. As you extend your healing to others, acknowledge that their struggles might be masked by layers of pain and loneliness. Providing a listening ear, a comforting word, or a gesture of understanding creates a nurturing environment for healing, fostering connection and resilience in adversity. Through acts of kindness and empathy, you become a guiding light in the darkness, leading the way toward wholeness for those lost in the shadows.

Conclusion

As we reach the end of this journey of embracing and healing your wounded inner child, it is essential to reflect on the significant transformations you have undergone and the profound changes you have initiated within yourself. The book served as a comprehensive guide, offering insights into understanding and addressing deep-seated wounds stemming from childhood trauma. By delving into each chapter, you have gained valuable knowledge and tools to cultivate a healthier and more integrated sense of self.

Exploring your inner child stands as the cornerstone of this healing process. Childhood trauma often casts a lingering shadow over your adult life, leading to emotional distress and **maladaptive** behaviors. Recognizing the origins and manifestations of trauma is key to comprehending its impact on your present self. By unraveling these origins, you have acquired a deeper understanding of how various traumas shape your adulthood, guiding you toward areas that necessitate healing. Acknowledgment and acceptance mark the initial steps on the path to healing. Creating a safe and nurturing space for your healing journey is crucial, as is fostering self-compassion as a fundamental element in inner healing. You've also learned the importance and value of engaging in self-compassionate practices like mindfulness and self-kindness, which serve as a soothing remedy for your wounded inner child, offering comfort and reassurance.

We also delved into practices such as mirror work, heartfelt journaling, and creative engagements to reconnect with your inner child, reviving a neglected bond. Revisiting cherished memories and reconnecting with childhood friends play a vital role in this process, facilitating the retrieval of lost aspects of yourself due to past trauma.

Healing through re-parenting, as **elucidated** in Chapter 4, involves addressing the negative self-perception stemming from childhood trauma. Establishing a strong foundation of self-care and engaging in compassionate dialogue with your inner child aids in rebuilding self-worth. Setting boundaries also becomes an act of self-love and respect, ensuring that your inner child feels secure and protected. Overcoming the obstacles entails confronting fears and acknowledging the role of resistance in the healing journey. By challenging resistance and breaking free from self-sabotaging patterns, you take significant steps towards embracing change and excel at preparing for rebirth and personal restoration. This chapter empowers you to dismantle barriers hindering your progress, fostering a mindset of resilience and adaptability.

The focus later shifts to repairing relationships and delving into patterns linked to unresolved trauma. Addressing issues like relationship OCD, commitment challenges, and infidelity emphasizes the significance of forgiveness and the pathway to establishing healthy connections. By unraveling these relational dynamics, you pave the way for more engaging and stable relationships.

We then reached parts of the book that center on the maintenance of inner child healing by integrating lessons and practices into your daily life. Continuous growth, self-discovery, and navigating setbacks gracefully become pivotal aspects of this journey toward healing. Here I provided strategies for sustaining the progress achieved and ensuring a lifelong commitment to your healing journey.

Lastly, Chapter 8 invites you to embrace a life of joy and wholeness. Rediscovering joy in your life signifies the transformative work you have undertaken. The journey towards wholeness, characterized by heightened self-awareness, emotional resilience, and inner peace, enables you to live authentically. Embracing newfound wholeness propels you towards a harmonious and enriching life experience that not only increases the meaning it has for you but is also a fantastic example for those around you. As you proceed on this journey, remember that healing is not a linear process but an ongoing evolution. Each step taken towards understanding and nurturing your inner child brings you closer to a life filled with joy and wholeness. The tools and insights gleaned from this book are meant to guide you, encouraging a compassionate and loving embrace of your true self. Your previously wounded inner child can now thrive in the nurturing environment you have cultivated, leading to a more harmonious and enriched life.

A Message of Hope

I implore you to pause and recognize the profound journey you have embarked upon. Embracing and healing your wounded inner child is a bold and transformative venture, demanding introspection, patience, and resilience. This expedition goes beyond simply healing old wounds; it is about reclaiming your entirety and fully embracing your authentic self. The process of healing your inner child may have illuminated hidden pains and unresolved emotions. Nevertheless, it has also unveiled your immense potential for growth, love, and self-compassion. You have come to understand and confront the origins of your trauma, nurture your inner child, and implement practical strategies for ongoing self-care and healing. Each step taken reflects your resilience and dedication to a healthier and more fulfilling life.

Healing is an ongoing journey where setbacks and moments of doubt are inevitable. Yet, these instances do not diminish your progress; they present opportunities for deeper growth and understanding. Every experience, whether challenging or uplifting, contributes to your continuous path of healing and self-discovery.

As you proceed on this path, remember the significance of *self-compassion*. Treat yourself with the same care and kindness you would extend to a beloved friend. Acknowledge your accomplishments, no matter how small, and celebrate your advancements. Your inner child thrives on love and acceptance, and genuine healing is fostered through acts of self-compassion. Seek support when needed, as healing is not a solitary pursuit. Surround yourself with a caring network of individuals who empathize with and validate your journey. Sharing your thoughts and emotions can offer comfort, insight, and encouragement, reinforcing the understanding that you are not alone. Look ahead with optimism and hope.

The knowledge and practices acquired from this book are not solely for addressing past wounds; they are tools for cultivating a life brimming with joy, authenticity, and fulfillment. By consistently applying the techniques discussed, you nurture a resilient and compassionate relationship with yourself, empowering you to confront future challenges with confidence and grace.

Imagine a future where your inner child thrives in a safe, loving environment and expresses themselves freely. Imagine a life where each day is embraced with eagerness and gratitude, where relationships are wholesome and rewarding, and your aspirations are pursued with assurance and delight. This envisioned future is not distant but a tangible reality that you actively shape through your healing journey.

Hold onto the hope that has guided you thus far. Trust in your capacity to heal, grow, and flourish. Your journey is unique, as is your resilience. Embrace each step with courage and an open heart, recognizing that every effort made toward healing is a profound expression of self-love. Your inner child embodies immense wisdom and creativity, and by nurturing this aspect of yourself, you unlock the potential for a life overflowing with joy and fulfillment.

As you progress, let hope illuminate your path. Believe in the transformative power of healing. Your once-wounded inner child is now on a quest toward wholeness, and with each passing day, you evolve into the individual you were destined to be. Embrace this **expedition** with hope, knowing that a brighter, more loving future eagerly awaits you!

Glossary

Adaptive: Able to adjust easily to unfamiliar situations and surroundings.

Affinity: An inherent liking of something or someone.

Agoraphobia: A type of anxiety disorder that encompasses an intense fear of going to public places.

Alleviate: To lessen the severity of something, like pain.

Amygdala: A section in our brain responsible for regulating emotions.

Animosity: Intense opposition to something or someone. Often falls into the bracket of hostility.

Anguish: Intense and continuous suffering. It can be mental or physical pain.

Beratement: Being aggressively or angrily scolded by another person.

Byproduct: Something that develops through the effects of something else. Usually referring to chemical or manufacturing processes.

Cardiovascular: Anything that relates to the functions of the heart.

Castigation: An extreme form of criticizing or punishing someone.

Catalyst: Something that acts as the force that sets off a specific event or person.

Catastrophizing: Refers to envisioning the worst possible outcome of an event.

Chastising: The act of severely reprimanding or scolding someone.

Cognitive Stimulation: Refers to anything that challenges brain functionality and promotes mental growth.

Compulsive: Refers to an inherent urge to do something despite a conscious desire not to act.

Complexities: Refers to any detailed intricacies or complications.

Condemnation: Refers to an act of intense disapproval.

Conducive: Assisting in the process of ensuring a specific situation meets its means.

Consensual: Relates to anything that is mutually agreed upon or to.

Conviction: Involves a strong, unshakeable opinion of something.

Crudely: Generally refers to behavior or speech that lacks civility or sophistication.

Curative: Something that cures another thing or restores health.

Decipher: To divulge a hidden meaning of something that's meaning isn't straightforward.

Deduce: Refers to drawing a conclusion about something.

Depreciation: The gradual reduction in the quality or value of something.

Deplete: To use something until there's nothing left. Generally, it refers to resources.

Deprived: Being prevented from having something.

Detrimental: Refers to something that causes damage or harm.

Dissipate: The act of becoming less or causing something to disperse.

Dissociation: Involves being separated or disconnected from something.

Distinguished: Refers to something that commands admiration and authority as a result of success.

Distorted: Changed out of a typical shape into something strange or incorrect.

Dominion: The state of control over something or someone.

Dormant: Refers to being in a state of stillness or inactivity.

Dumbfounded: To be in a state of intense surprise or astonishment.

Elucidated: Refers to something that is clearly explained.

Endeavor: Refers to the act of trying to achieve something.

Ensue: The reaction of something that follows another event.

Encompasses: Refers to what something covers or includes.

Euphoria: The feeling of intense pleasure or happiness.

Expedition: An organized trip undertaken by a group of people with a shared purpose in mind.

Exploit: The act of benefiting from a resource to its full extent, generally more than what is acceptable.

Estranged: Refers to the state of being distanced from or no longer connected to someone, resulting in emotional distance.

Fruition: The process of an idea or project playing out as envisioned, leading to its fulfillment.

Fundamentally: Refers to the core or key aspects of a subject or situation.

Hinder: To prevent or slow down progress or create obstacles, generally resulting in delays or obstructions.

Hyper-alertness: The condition or state of being excessively aware, vigilant, or unusually attentive to your surroundings.

Inadequacy: Refers to the state or quality of not measuring up to something or lacking in what is required.

Imbalanced: Refers to a state of unequal proportion or lacking balance; uneven in distribution.

Incoherent: Not being coherent or in a state of unity, resulting in disjointed or disconnected information or results.

Inevitably: Refers to something that is bound to happen, meaning it's unavoidable no matter what.

Inadvertently: Accidentally or done without conscious intention, implying actions taken unknowingly.

Incessant: Refers to continuance without interruption; something that is constant and persistent.

Inexplicable: Refers to when something cannot be explained or rationalized; generally, it defies comprehension.

Impede: To delay or prevent the progress of someone or something by creating hindrances or barriers.

Impenetrable: Refers to something that cannot be passed through or penetrated, indicating something's integrity cannot be breached.

Immerse: To involve oneself in a particular activity, subject, or interest fully and completely.

Instilled: The gradual but firm establishment of an idea, belief, or perception in someone's mind.

Intervention: The act or process of involving something in order to modify, change, or influence a situation or a person's behavior.

Intrusive: Refers to something that causes disruption or annoyance, as it is usually unwelcome or uninvited.

Introspect: To reflect on and evaluate your own feelings, thoughts, or inner consciousness.

Liberation: Refers to the act of setting something free. Can be from oppression, imprisonment, or constraints.

Manifest: Refers to something that becomes clearly visible or evident and can be easily perceived or understood.

Manifestation: An event that clearly represents or embodies an abstract concept or idea.

Martyring: Refers to the act of immense sacrifice or suffering for the sake of someone or something else.

Meticulous: The act or habit of impressive precision and attention to detail when busy with tasks.

Morphs: Changes distinctly from one shape or form to another.

Multifaceted: Consisting of various different aspects and elements; something that varies in nature.

Mutilated: Something that is severely damaged or injured to the point of disfigurement or abnormality.

Neurons: Nerve cells in the brain responsible for transmitting information throughout the nervous system.

Nostalgia: Refers to a sentimental yearning or affectionate longing for experiences from the past and often relates to fond, meaningful memories.

Peculiar: Distinctively different, uncommon, or strange.

Perceived: Refers to noticing, understanding, or becoming aware of something through knowledge or observation.

Perpetual: When something goes on for a long time, without interruption or breaks, it feels eternal.

Precarious: Something uncertain or unstable; can feel likely to fall or collapse.

Preconceived: Formed or shaped beforehand, often without having all the evidence or information available; usually referring to values and ideas.

Prevalent: Found in many places or occurring in a specific space or at a specific time; commonly found or widespread.

Precedence: Refers to being considered more important or having priority over someone or something else.

Procrastination: The act of delaying or postponing tasks, usually through engaging in unnecessary delays or inefficiencies.

Prodigy: A person, usually someone young, who possesses exceptional abilities or qualities at a young age.

Prolonged: Something that goes on for an extended period of time, longer than usual or expected; lasting for a considerable amount of time.

Promiscuity: The common practice of engaging in frequent sexual activity with multiple partners or without being carefully selective in choosing a partner.

Psychotherapist: A professional who employs psychological methods to treat mental health disorders as opposed to medical interventions.

Psyche: Our core beings, souls, or minds that encompass our consciousness, thoughts, and emotions.

Quirks: Refers to habits or aspects of someone's character that are regarded as unusual or eccentric.

Rationalizing: The act of attempting to justify or explain something using logical reasons.

Reciprocate: Returning an action, gesture, or feeling initiated by someone or something else.

Reconcile: Refers to making peace or returning to a state of friendliness following a conflict.

Redefine: Refers to the act of changing the definition of something that contradicts its initial definition.

Regulate: Refers to controlling or adjusting the rate, speed, or functioning of a machine or process to ensure it operates as intended.

Reparation: To repair something. The act of making amends after wrongdoing or harm done to someone.

Repose: A state of tranquility, rest, sleep, peacefulness, and relaxation in nature.

Reprimanded: Scolding or rebuking someone for perceived bad or inappropriate behavior.

Repressing: The act of suppressing or restraining something, usually by force or through mental exertion.

Revelation: An enlightening, shocking, or formerly unknown fact or piece of information, typically revealed in a dramatic or unexpected way.

Sentimental: Referring to something that is prompted by, characterized by, or appeals to emotions, tenderness, or nostalgia.

Schizophrenia: A mental disorder characterized by abnormal or failed communication between various parts of thought processes, resulting in a distorted way of perceiving or understanding things.

Self-loathing: Extreme hatred, disgust, dislike, or any negative feelings directed towards oneself.

Solace: Refers to comfort, relief, or consolation in a stressful or emotionally draining time.

Stagnant: When something isn't moving or flowing, often leading to a lack of progress or growth; refers to inactivity.

Stigma: A widespread belief in something or someone, usually involving shame, disgrace, or any negative association attached to it.

Suffused: To gradually fill or spread with a particular emotion or quality.

Summation: The process of adding up or summarizing information or details to create a comprehensive overview.

Torment: Severe physical or mental suffering, anguish, or distress caused by pain.

Transcends: Goes beyond the limits or boundaries of something, surpassing or exceeding what is expected or known.

Transpired: Refers to something that occurred or happened, usually as a part of a sequence of events.

Traverse: To travel across, move through, or navigate a particular environment or terrain.

Tumult: This refers to a chaotic situation or loud, chaotic noise or disturbance, often caused by a large group of people.

Unraveling: Refers to resolving a complex or puzzling situation, typically revealing hidden details or solving mysteries.

Venture: An exciting or daring journey or undertaking involving uncertainty and potential challenges.

Victimization: The act of being subjected to or singling out someone for cruel, unfair, or unjust treatment.

Xenophobia: Deep-seated dislike or prejudice against people from other countries or cultures, usually caused by fear or ignorance.

Yanked: Refers to being abruptly or forcibly pulled with a swift, sudden movement or jerking motion.

References

BetterHelp Editorial Team. (n.d.). *Healing your inner child: Tips and techniques*. BetterHelp. https://www.betterhelp.com/advice/parenting/healing-your-inner-child-tips-and-techniques/

Boerger, L. (2022, January 25). *22 ways to connect with your inner child*. Made with Lemons. https://madewithlemons.co/connect-with-your-inner-child/

Brooten-Brooks, M. C. (n.d.). *How to set healthy boundaries with anyone*. Verywell Health. https://www.verywellhealth.com/setting-boundaries-5208802

Burney, R. (n.d.). *The recovery process for inner child healing - through the fear*. Heal Your Inner Child. https://www.healyourinnerchild.com/book-content/the-recovery-process-for-inner-child-healing-through-the-fear

Charlie Health Editorial Team. (2023, May 25). *How to heal your inner child*. Charlie Health; Charlie Health. https://www.charliehealth.com/post/how-to-heal-your-inner-child

Chelsie. (2022, August 15). *Fun ways to connect with your inner child*. Relationship Enrichment Center. https://www.relationshipenrichmentcenter.com/blog/2022/fun-ways-to-connect-with-your-inner-child

Cherry, K. (n.d.). *How listening to music can have psychological benefits*. Verywell Mind; Verywell Mind. https://www.verywellmind.com/surprising-psychological-benefits-of-music-4126866

Childs Heyl, J. (n.d.). *Inner child work: How your past shapes your present*. Verywell Mind. https://www.verywellmind.com/inner-child-work-how-your-past-shapes-your-present-7152929

Cortisol. (n.d.). Cleveland Clinic. https://my.clevelandclinic.org/health/articles/22187-cortisol

Cronkleton, E. (n.d.). *10 breathing exercises to try when you're feeling stressed.* Healthline. https://www.healthline.com/health/breathing-exercise#pursed-lip-breathing

Cycling - health benefits. (n.d.). Better Health Channel. https://www.betterhealth.vic.gov.au/health/HealthyLiving/cycling-health-benefits

Das, T. (2023, August 7). *Inner child patterns that hijack our adult relationships.* Hindustan Times. https://www.hindustantimes.com/lifestyle/relationships/inner-child-patterns-that-hijack-our-adult-relationships-101691382852046.html

Davis, S. (2020, July 27). *Reparenting to Heal the Wounded Inner Child.* CPTSD Foundation.org. https://cptsdfoundation.org/2020/07/27/reparenting-to-heal-the-wounded-inner-child/

Dissociation and dissociative disorders. (n.d.). Better Health Channel. https://www.betterhealth.vic.gov.au/health/conditionsandtreatments/dissociation-and-dissociative-disorders

Ellen | EKT Creatives-Spiritual Business Girlie. (2022, November 22). *Best mindfulness exercises to mend your inner child.* Medium. https://medium.com/@ektcreatives/mindfulness-meditation-to-heal-inner-child-75d2ec4f882f

51 inner child journaling prompts. (2021, June 8). Nottai. https://nottai.com/blogs/journaling/51-inner-child-journaling-prompts

Ford, D. (2021, July 16). *Reparenting your inner child: Ways to encourage therapeutic dialogue.* Step up for Mental Health. https://www.stepupformentalhealth.org/reparenting-your-inner-child/

Ford, R. D. (2023, December 19). *What is inner child work and how does it contribute to personal growth and healing?* Reggie D. Ford.

https://reggiedford.com/what-is-inner-child-work-and-how-does-it-contribute-to-personal-growth-and-healing/

Four techniques for practicing self-compassion. (2023, July 25). Cleveland Clinic. https://health.clevelandclinic.org/self-compassion

Gillis, K. (2022, February 19). *10 ways childhood trauma can manifest in adult relationships.* Psychology Today. https://www.psychologytoday.com/za/blog/invisible-bruises/202202/10-ways-childhood-trauma-can-manifest-in-adult-relationships

Goldstein, E. (n.d.). *What is an inner child and what does it know.* Integrative Psychotherapy & Trauma Treatment. https://integrativepsych.co/new-blog/what-is-an-inner-child

Griffiths, N. (n.d.). *30 Journal Prompts for Inner Child Healing and Shadow Work.* Seeking Serotonin. https://seekingserotonin.com/journal-prompts-for-inner-child-healing/?utm_content=cmp-true

How to overcome fear of change: 8 ways to navigate the unknown. (n.d.). Calm Blog. https://www.calm.com/blog/fear-of-change

How your childhood influences your present in adulthood: What you can do about it. (n.d.). Psychology Everywhere. https://psychologyeverywhere.com/articles/how-your-childhood-influences-your-present-in-adulthood-what-you-can-do-about-it/

Inner child healing: Reclaiming joy and wholeness. (n.d.). The Human Beauty Movement. Retrieved June 1, 2024, from https://thehumanbeautymovement.com/inner-child-healing-reclaiming-joy-and-wholeness/

Inner child work: How to heal by reparenting yourself. (n.d.). Big Self School. https://www.bigselfschool.com/post/inner-child-work

Johnson, T. (2022, October 11). *8 tips for healing your inner child.* Choosing Therapy. https://www.choosingtherapy.com/inner-child-healing/

Juma, J. (2023, March 23). *Making the most of your setbacks and challenges.* LinkedIn. https://www.linkedin.com/pulse/making-most-your-setbacks-challenges-juneyoung-juma/

Just keep swimming: 9 health benefits of water workouts. (2023, August 14). Cleveland Clinic. https://health.clevelandclinic.org/swimming-joint-friendly-and-good-for-the-heart

Kampgrounds of America. (2023, May 8). *12 benefits of camping | why camping is good for you.* Kampgrounds of America. https://koa.com/blog/the-benefits-of-camping-why-camping-is-good-for-you/

Kekos, B. (2023, September 29). *What is the inner child? The unconscious part of your mind that holds your unmet childhood needs.* Brainz. https://www.brainzmagazine.com/post/what-is-the-inner-child-the-unconscious-part-of-your-mind-that-holds-your-unmet-childhood-needs

Kelly, O. (n.d.). *Identifying and coping with relationship OCD.* Verywell Mind. https://www.verywellmind.com/ocd-and-romantic-relationships-2510557

Kennedy, J. J. (2023, October 17). *Embracing change and conquering fear.* Psychology Today. https://www.psychologytoday.com/us/blog/brain-reboot/202310/embracing-change-and-conquering-fear

LaPorte, D. (2020, May 5). *How your relationship with your inner child affects every part of your life.* Medium. https://daniellelaporte.medium.com/how-your-relationship-with-your-inner-child-affects-every-part-of-your-life-5ef8773711f4

Lash, K. (2024, March 15). *Find Self-Growth Through Inner Child Healing.* SpiritQuest Sedona Retreats. https://retreatsinsedona.com/blog/heal-the-inner-child-for-self-growth/

LeClair, C. (2023, April 26). *Is your inner child doing the talking?* LinkedIn. https://www.linkedin.com/pulse/your-inner-child-doing-talking-cassandra-leclair-ph-d-

Mandriota, M. (n.d.). *How to cope with the fear of change.* Verywell Mind. https://www.verywellmind.com/i-fear-change-how-to-cope-with-the-unknown-5189851

Markle, P. S. (2017, April 14). *Your inner child needs to believe feeling leads to healing.* Medium. https://paul-markle.medium.com/rediscover-your-inner-child-b8abb5aa3038

Matheka, W. (2023, March 18). *Journal Prompts for Inner Child Healing.* Wendy Matheka. https://www.wendymatheka.com/post/journal-prompts-for-inner-child-healing

Miller, J. (2021, April 23). *How reconnecting with our inner child increases our happiness.* Thrive Global. https://community.thriveglobal.com/how-reconnecting-with-our-inner-child-increases-our-happiness/

Miretti, V. (n.d.). *Our inner child and how it impacts our love life.* Victoria Miretti. https://victoriamiretti.com/our-inner-child-and-how-it-impacts-our-love-life-webinar/

Moore, C. (2019, June 2). *How to practice self-compassion: 8 techniques and tips.* Positive Psychology. https://positivepsychology.com/how-to-practice-self-compassion/

N.C. Division of Social Services and the Family and Children's Resource Program. (2012, May). *How Trauma Affects Child Brain Development.* Practice Notes.org. https://practicenotes.org/v17n2/brain.htm

Niedra, A. (n.d.). *How to set boundaries consciously.* Voice Dialogue in Daily Life. https://www.voicedialogue.com/how-to-set-boundaries-more-consciously/

Nostalgic Italian. (2019, December 20). *Fear and the Inner Child.* Various Ramblings of a Nostalgic Italian. https://nostalgicitalian.com/2019/12/20/fear-and-the-inner-child/

OmScape. (2023, August 4). *Nurturing your inner child: A path to healing and mindfulness in the metaverse.* LinkedIn. https://linkedin.com/pulse/nurturing-your-inner-child-path-healing-mindfulness-metaverse?trk=public_post_main-feed-card_feed-article-content

Pawar Chavan, D. K. (2023, November 4). *10 exercises to heal your inner child and why you need to heal yourself.* Medium. https://medium.com/@drketaki.oms/10-exercises-to-heal-your-inner-child-and-why-you-need-to-heal-yourself-d9bae1a1ec6a

Pedersen, T., & Smith, J. (n.d.). *10 exercises to heal your inner child.* Psych Central. https://psychcentral.com/health/how-to-heal-your-inner-child

Randolph Pitman, K. (2011, March 7). *Softening the resistance that arises when you want to change.* Growing Human Kindness. https://growinghumankindness.com/resistant-to-helping-yourself/

Raypole, C. (n.d.). *8 ways to start healing your inner child.* Healthline. https://www.healthline.com/health/mental-health/inner-child-healing

Raypole, C. (2020, June 26). *Finding and getting to know your inner child.* Healthline. https://www.healthline.com/health/inner-child

Robinson, L., Smith, M., Segal, J., & Shubin, J. (n.d.). *The benefits of play for adults.* HelpGuide.org. https://www.helpguide.org/articles/mental-health/benefits-of-play-for-adults.htm

Rojas, C. (2023, April 13). Conversations with our inner child. Medium; Age of Awareness. https://medium.com/age-of-awareness/conversations-with-our-inner-child-2920231c0c34

Rosennab. (2019, September 17). *How to heal childhood trauma without forgiving the person who caused it.* Medium; The Startup. https://medium.com/swlh/how-to-heal-childhood-trauma-without-forgiving-the-person-who-caused-it-e83ac9e0c5a1

Saluja, K. (2023, November 24). *Embracing the inner child: A journey of self-discovery and healing with alice miller.* Medium. https://medium.com/@kulwantsaluja/embracing-the-inner-child-a-journey-of-self-discovery-and-healing-with-alice-miller-eee3ccfdecf4

Saluja, K. (2024, February 24). *Embracing the inner child for healing and wholeness*. Medium. https://medium.com/@kulwantsaluja/embracing-the-inner-child-for-healing-and-wholeness-780f4c65104e

Santos-Longhurst, A. (n.d.). *What are the symptoms and causes of high cortisol levels?* Healthline. https://www.healthline.com/health/high-cortisol-symptoms#symptoms

Sharma, S. (n.d.). *The power of forgiveness in the process of inner healing*. Life Coach Sangeeta. https://www.coachsangeeta.com/the-power-of-forgiveness-in-the-process-of-inner-healing/

Sutton, J. (2022, October 8). *Inner child healing: 35 practical tools for growing beyond your past*. Positive Psychology. https://positivepsychology.com/inner-child-healing/

Tabac, M. (2023, March 14). *Embracing the fears of your inner child*. LinkedIn. https://www.linkedin.com/pulse/embracing-fears-your-inner-child-magda-tabac-

Tan, B. (n.d.). *How understanding your inner child can help your adult relationships*. Kopi Date. https://www.explore.kopidate.com/how-understanding-your-inner-child-can-help-your-adult-relationships

Thalia. (2022, June 13). *How to embrace your inner child and find joy*. Notes by Thalia; Notes By Thalia. https://notesbythalia.com/embrace-your-inner-child-and-find-joy/

The hidden impact of trauma on self-esteem: Understanding the connection. (2023, May 12). Khiron Clinics. https://khironclinics.com/blog/the-hidden-impact-of-trauma-on-self-esteem-understanding-the-connection/

The long-term effects of childhood trauma on mental health. (2024, April 11). ImPossible Psychological Services. https://www.impossiblepsychservices.com.sg/our-resources/articles/2024/04/11/the-long-term-effects-of-childhood-trauma-on-mental-health

The science of journaling: How writing benefits your brain. (n.d.). Shaka Tribe. https://shakatribeshop.com/pages/the-science-of-journaling-how-writing-benefits-your-brain

Trauma types. (n.d.). The National Child Traumatic Stress Network. https://www.nctsn.org/what-is-child-trauma/trauma-types

Tuttle, C. (n.d.). *"What's wrong with me?" Why you resist doing the healing work.* Carol Tuttle. https://ct.liveyourtruth.com/whats-wrong-with-me-resistance-to-doing-healing/

Understanding child trauma. (n.d.). Substance Abuse and Mental Health Services Administration. https://www.samhsa.gov/child-trauma/understanding-child-trauma

Understanding your inner child. (2023, April 29). Psychotherapy Kuchenna. https://www.psychotherapykuchenna.com/2023/04/29/understanding-your-inner-child/

Virro, K. (2020, August 24). *Harmful myths about boundaries.* Fresh Insight. https://www.fresh-insight.ca/post/harmful-myths-about-boundaries

West, M. (2022, April 21). *Guided imagery: Techniques, benefits, and more.* Medical News Today. https://www.medicalnewstoday.com/articles/guided-imagery

What are the 13 types of childhood trauma and why you should know it. (2023, March 17). Roots through Recovery. https://roots-recovery.com/what-are-the-13-types-of-childhood-trauma-and-why-you-should-know-it/

What does a healthy relationship look like? (n.d.). New York State. https://www.ny.gov/teen-dating-violence-awareness-and-prevention/what-does-healthy-relationship-look

Image References

Abobo. (2014). *G-e-m the climb mountain girl joy*. In Pixabay.
https://pixabay.com/photos/g-e-m-the-climb-mountain-girl-joy-
1115537/

Admartdigital. (2018). *Woman people adult lifestyle young*. In Pixabay.
https://pixabay.com/photos/woman-people-adult-lifestyle-young-
3157462/

Annie Spratt. (2020). *Black and red floral happy birthday signage*. In Unsplash.
https://unsplash.com/photos/black-and-red-floral-happy-birthday-
signage-WQC8HvAU2SY

Brett Jordan. (2021). *Brown wooden blocks on white surface*. In Unsplash.
https://unsplash.com/photos/brown-wooden-blocks-on-white-
surface-NjILic_dUVI

Caleb Woods. (2016). *Girl covering her face with both hands*. In Unsplash.
https://unsplash.com/photos/girl-covering-her-face-with-both-
hands-VZILDYoqn_U

D_alexander33. (2020). *Mexico cave cenote sinkhole maya*. In Pixabay.
https://pixabay.com/photos/mexico-cave-cenote-sinkhole-maya-
5066180/

DesignCologist. (2018). *Two women kneeling under falling confetti*. In Unsplash.
https://unsplash.com/photos/two-women-kneeling-under-falling-
confetti-y91FmfcmYYw

Edge2Edge Media. (2020). *Person holding white round ornament*. In Unsplash.
https://unsplash.com/photos/person-holding-white-round-
ornament-vwLgsQx5d2Y

Efe Kurnaz. (2017). *Multicolored hallway*. In Unsplash.
https://unsplash.com/photos/multicolored-hallway-RnCPiXixooY

Gabby Orcutt. (2016). *Adult and girl holding forever scrabble letters during daytime*. In
Unsplash. https://unsplash.com/photos/adult-and-girl-holding-
forever-scrabble-letters-during-daytime-kPtrg4Z6jZ0

Geralt. (2019). *Hands give particles energy*. In Pixabay. https://pixabay.com/photos/hands-give-particles-energy-3753417/

Md Samir Sayek. (2023). *A person sitting on a chair in front of a window*. In Unsplash. https://unsplash.com/photos/a-person-sitting-on-a-chair-in-front-of-a-window-PPxtBAGVie8

Melissa Askew. (2018). *Girl sitting on daisy flowerbed in forest*. In Unsplash. https://unsplash.com/photos/girl-sitting-on-daisy-flowerbed-in-forest-8n00CqwnqO8

Monstera Production. (2021). *Black mother with daughter drinking water from glasses*. In Pexels. https://www.pexels.com/photo/black-mother-with-daughter-drinking-water-from-glasses-7114373/

Ninosouza. (2019). *People friends together happy kid*. In Pixabay. https://pixabay.com/photos/people-friends-together-happy-kid-4050698/

PublicCo. (2017). *Ocean sunset person silhouette*. In Pixabay. https://pixabay.com/photos/ocean-sunset-person-silhouette-2203720/

PublicDomainPictures. (2012). *Chains feet sand bondage prison*. In Pixabay. https://pixabay.com/photos/chains-feet-sand-bondage-prison-19176/

Thomas Wolter. (2019). *Ear mouth nose face head voices*. In Pixabay. https://pixabay.com/photos/ear-mouth-nose-face-head-voices-3971050/

Tim Mossholder. (2017). *You are worthy of love sign beside tree and road*. In Unsplash. https://unsplash.com/photos/you-are-worthy-of-love-sign-beside-tree-and-road-SR8ByN6xY3k

Warren. (2017). *Photo of person holding lighted sparkler*. In Unsplash. https://unsplash.com/photos/photo-of-person-holding-lighted-sparkler-kMRMcUcO81M

www.ingramcontent.com/pod-product-compliance
Lightning Source LLC
Chambersburg PA
CBHW051315120626
46547CB00015B/2250

*9 7989 9080 4692 *